Advance Praise for the

"This book

simply instructional a

East Side. It is a super

of the impact of Afric

Italian, and Jewish im

Chinese sailors and m

and lived on the Lowe

City. That neighborho

grandmother lived in

the place where the a

us learned what it me

The book is chock-ful

descriptions, and folk

impossible to put dow

the entire book.

—*Edward I. Koch*

"Any guide book to the Lower East Side of
Manhattan that acknowledges Lorenzo Da
Ponte, Ira Aldridge, Henry James, and Emma
Goldman—absent the usual 'huddled masses'
or the 'wretched refuse' of anyone's 'teeming
shores'—is by definition a joy and
an education."

—*Senator Daniel Patrick Moynihan*

Six HERITAGE TOURS

OF THE
LOWER EAST SIDE

RUTH LIMMER

A WALKING GUIDE
IN COLLABORATION WITH NYC'S

**LOWER EAST SIDE
TENEMENT MUSEUM**

NEW YORK UNIVERSITY PRESS
NEW YORK AND LONDON

NEW YORK UNIVERSITY PRESS

New York and London

©1997 by New York University

Map Design ©1997 by Roher/Sprague Partners

Map Illustrations ©1997 by Barbara Morse

Library of Congress Cataloging-in-Publication Data

Limmer, Ruth.
    Six heritage tours of the Lower East Side : a walking guide
/ Ruth Limmer in collaboration with NYC's Lower East Side
Tenement Museum.
        p.   cm.
    Includes bibliographical references (p.   ) and index.
    ISBN 0-8147-5130-X (alk. paper)
    1. Lower East Side (New York, N.Y.)—Tours.
    2. New York (N.Y.)—Tours
    3. Walking—New York (State)—New York—Guidebooks.
    4. Minorities—New York (State)—New York—History—
    Pictorial works.
    F128.18.L53   1997
    917.47'10443—dc21   97-2074
                                         CIP

Book Design by Melanie Roher,
Roher/Sprague Partners

Manufactured in the United States of America

10 9 8 7 6 5 4 3 2 1

Contents

Only for the egotist and the dogmatist…is there one "history" only. The rest of us live with the suspicion that there are as many histories as there are people and maybe a few more—

Robert Coover,
Whatever Happened to Gloomy Gus of the Chicago Bears?

Acknowledgments

This book—brainchild of Ruth Abram, founder and president of the Lower East Side Tenement Museum—is a collaborative affair which began as a series of walking tours under the auspices of the Museum. With the generous support of Furthermore, a publication project of the J. M. Kaplan Fund, Sherrill Wilson chose the sites and prepared the African tour; Annette Bus the German; Peter Kwong the Chinese; Betty Boyd Caroli the Italian; and Seth Kamil, from sites suggested by Jenna Joselit, prepared the Eastern European Jewish tour. I expanded on their work, leaning heavily on the works cited in the bibliography. Additional researcher/scholars then came aboard to further expand, to clarify, and sometimes to contradict. Elizabeth L. Grossi allowed me to read her thesis on first-generation African-American leaders, prepared for a master's degree in history from Hunter College; Debra Bach and Stanley Nadel examined the German chapter; Vernon Takeshita the Chinese; Ed O'Donnell the Irish and Italian; and Naomi W. Cohen critiqued a partial draft of the Jewish chapter. Raya Barut assisted with translations. None of them have read the final version and are therefore not responsible for any errors which my further research may have added.

The illustrations were located by Anita Jacobson, then curator of the Lower East Side Tenement Museum, with the assistance of Sara Moy and Steve Long, who verified addresses and locations. The guide would not have been possible without them. Nor would it have been so handsomely displayed without the maps drawn by Barbara Morse and the skills of the design team of Roher/Sprague Partners, specifically the long-suffering Sue Ann Sprague and my long-time collaborator on *Tenement Times*, Melanie Roher.

In today's climate, sharpened ethnic sensibilities and new historical approaches demand attention. I take full responsibility for emphases and interpretations should any offend.

Ruth Limmer

How to Use This Book

Each heritage chapter begins with a map showing the location of each numbered site in the tour that follows. Each map also shows subway lines (S) and bus routes (M or B) useful for the start and end of each tour. Some maps also mark the site of the **LOWER EAST SIDE TENEMENT MUSEUM**, at 97 Orchard Street, where visitors can walk the halls, check out the toilet facilities, and visit the authentic living quarters of people who once actually lived on the streets covered in these tours.

Probably the best way to use the book, if you intend to walk from site to site, is to prepare—as any good traveler should—by at-home reading. The introductions to the tours—the heritage chapters—provide a brief history of each of the six groups covered in the guide.

Some tour sites overlap. A church called to your attention in the Irish chapter, for example, may also have been attended by Italians some decades later. Usually there is a cross reference in the text to tell you so. Take that occasion to read about an ethnic group unfamiliar to you.

No tour requires that you follow the order of the stops. If you wish, start from the opposite end or anywhere in the middle. You are not trailing after a tour leader who herds you briskly from monument to monument. And no tour requires completion in one visit; in fact, there is no way to estimate how long any tour will take. Ideally, you should think of yourself as a serious tourist in a foreign country; only the uncurious think they can get to know a city in an afternoon.

What else is to be seen on the block? What surprises does the neighborhood hold? Imagine what the street must have been like in the old days. Imagine yourself a newcomer, probably without English, without money, certainly without the sure knowledge that you can return to a different neighborhood at the end of the day. Have something to eat at a diner or from a vendor's cart. Take time to read the graffiti. Examine the architecture, the fire escapes, the cornices on the buildings; observe how the shadows fall.

Talk to people. Attend a church service. Check out the prices in the shops and perhaps buy something useful to remind you of your visit. If you wander away from locations on the map, and perhaps you should, don't consider yourself lost. Like the serious tourist, you are merely accumulating adventures to relate to the stay-at-homes.

But you needn't be a tourist on foot in order to enjoy and profit from this guide. Because it is still true that there is no frigate like a book, these heritage tours are also for those happily ensconced in armchairs. And once you have completed the tours on the page, read some of the books listed in the bibliography. Become your own expert on immigration, not just to New York's Lower East Side but to the whole country. The people discussed in these pages have descendants everywhere in America. They are us.

African Heritage

Manhattan Island had not yet been purchased from the Indians when the first
Africans arrived in the Dutch colony in 1625.
Between that year and the next, when the
Dutch West India Company founded New
Amsterdam, eleven men, probably slaves cap-
tured from Portuguese vessels en route from
Angola to Brazil, were put to work in the
growing settlement. The future New
Amsterdam needed strong backs to build its
fort, to plant and harvest its crops, and to
deliver pelts to its ships. And the director
general, Peter Stuyvesant, had need of
domestic servants.

Given what we know of slavery as it would
develop in the United States, the terms and
conditions of slavery during the Dutch years
were not horrendous. Lacking a specific policy
establishing slavery, the Dutch allowed their
slaves recourse to the law and permitted them
to attend and to marry in the Dutch Reform
Church (African women began arriving in
1627). And after a period of eighteen or nineteen years, the slaves were deeded land and
manumitted to "half freedom," which entailed
no more each year than providing their previous owners with bushels of farm harvest and
"one fat hog."

An African woman and man laboring for the Dutch in the busy port of New Amsterdam, c. 1643.

Five Points was an equal-opportunity slum to be inhabited by Africans, Irish, and Chinese. Few pictures of its worst streets exist because artists and, later, photographers were fearful of entering the notorious lair of thugs, thieves, and murderers.

The English system was both less benign and more far-reaching. Beginning in 1664, when the British annexed New Netherlands and renamed its major port New York, slavery became the dominant labor system in the colonies. Soon Africans (and Indians) were put under curfew and forbidden either to bear arms or to congregate on the streets. Most aggrieving, they were forced to toil without the expectation even of half freedom.

Although the first bill to abolish slavery in New York State was passed in 1799, it was not until July 4, 1827, that the last slaves in the state received freedom. Despite that, a commercially profitable slave trade survived in New York at least until 1849.

But even with freedom, blacks were not allowed to sit down in churches or courts. And their housing remained essentially segregated, in large measure limited to the Lower East Side in the slums of Five Points (named for what is now the intersection of Baxter Street, Worth Street, and Columbus Park) and to sections of the Sixth and Eighth wards (the political divisions of old New York resembling present-day councilmanic districts but holding unequal populations).

It is no wonder that in 1712, and again in 1741, the Africans staged uprisings. In the first case, the deaths of a few white men led to the execution of nineteen Africans and the community's loss of its right to own land. In the second case, due to conspiracy theories—Africans were thought to be plotting to burn down the colony—thirty blacks were executed and over twice that number deported.

But rebellion was not the only story: independent black businesses and churches were founded, mutual-aid societies were formed, and through the offices of the New York Manumission Society, the first of what would be six or seven African Free Schools [see stop #15] was established in 1787 to prepare youths for gainful employment.

The black population in Manhattan grew and waned. As recorded by the federal census of 1800, slaves and free people of color numbered 6,397—some 10 percent of the City's total population of sixty thousand. Ten years later, there were 7,470, of whom fewer than a sixth were enslaved. By 1840, more than sixteen thousand blacks lived in a city that had grown to over three hundred thousand. By mid-century, the number had dropped to thirteen thousand while the City itself had swollen to over half a million.

The drop in population was job related. Although there were many skilled artisans among them, as the economy of the City changed, most blacks were employed as servants or laborers (often as dockers or, like Sojourner Truth's son, as mariners). By mid-century, newly arrived Irishmen were increasingly favored for these jobs, and Irish women took over as domestics. Only 3 percent of black women still held household jobs by 1855, when, as Christine Stansell tells us in *City of Women*, "the availability of the Irish pushed black women…into specialized situations in the retinues of the wealthy and in brothels as laundresses, charwomen and maids."

There was, however, a small black middle class, increasingly strong and independent—doctors, lawyers, teachers, ministers, entrepreneurs. Through their churches (the chief

4

institution organizing social life), schools, and voluntary associations, they worked to serve the needs of their far poorer sisters and brothers.

But whether poverty-stricken or comfortably off, all blacks faced discrimination, segregation, and disenfranchisement. Some, like the college-educated journalist John Russwurm [see stop #12], left for Liberia a century before Marcus Garvey advocated a return to Africa. Others worked to change the situation through political action and self-help organizations.

Then, in 1861, the Civil War began. Two years later, Lincoln issued the Emancipation Proclamation. On February 6, 1863, Frederick Douglass, speaking at Cooper Union [see stop #3], hailed it as "the greatest event of the century—in our whole history." But on July 13, 1863, instead of continued celebration, came the great trauma: the Draft Riots.

Fury at the first federal draft in the nation's history—from which the well-to-do could escape by paying $300 or employing a substitute—coming atop inflation, wretched living conditions, and fear of job competition from the newly freed southern blacks, led the City's desperate immigrant underclass to riot and rampage. Instigated by the Irish, mobs burned down the Colored Orphan Asylum (Fifth Avenue and 43rd Street). The founding president of what would become Hunter College, an Irish immigrant himself and surely an eyewitness, Thomas Hunter described the scene in an unpublished novel:

Soon the red-forked flames shot out of every window as if they were living things. Determined to destroy whatever

None of the children died in the blaze set by the Draft rioters, but their orphanage was burned to the ground.

they touched, they crept along the cornice, they danced about the roof; and through the windows, they could be seen keeping up an infernal riot, jumping up and down, running here and there as if to find some spot that they had not yet destroyed. Then the roof fell in with a great crash, and for a moment it seemed as though the fire had been extinguished, but only for a moment. A great volume of black smoke ascended in spiral curves and intensified the darkness of the night. But the flames soon mastered the fallen debris, and shot up higher and fiercer and more triumphant than ever. The heavens were painted a yellowish red....In less than an hour the building—the refuge of poor helpless colored children—was one black mass of smoking ruins, and the mob dispersed, some to seek rest in cellar and garret and others to continue their work of robbery and destruction.

In the history textbook he wrote, Hunter elaborated on the "destruction": "They cut the telegraph wires, destroyed railroads, set fire…to several private houses, killed Negroes, wherever encountered, in the most barbarous way, hanging some of them to lamp posts."

Four days later, 125 people lay dead and perhaps as many as twelve hundred blacks and their supporters had been injured. What Hunter was to call the "most disgraceful event of the Civil War" ended an era. Blacks, if they could, fled to Brooklyn (still a city of its own) and upstate to towns like Yonkers and New Rochelle. Certainly few remained in the old wards of the Lower East Side.

Now the story becomes a prototypically New York one; it is about real estate.

Soon after the turn of the century, two construction projects coincided: on West 34th Street, where a pocket of blacks lived, massive new buildings were going up—among them Macy's department store and the Pennsylvania Railroad station. Meanwhile a new elevated train line was reaching from downtown Manhattan north to and along Lenox Avenue. Real estate development follows train tracks with the same inevitability as new construction ousts old residents.

Lenox Avenue was a major boulevard in an area that had been established in 1658 by Peter Stuyvesant. Called Nieuw Haarlem, it lay some ten miles north of New Amsterdam at the end of a road built by the colony's African slaves. Now it was called simply Harlem, and most of the land that had once been farmed had long since been transmuted into gracious residential streets of single-family brownstones firmly within the City.

As the newly accessible Harlem was being overbuilt and underrented, the displaced blacks of the West 34th Street area were seeking new places to live in their geographically segregated city. A prescient black real estate man made the connection. Thus a neighborhood inhabited largely by Jews and Italians who had escaped the Lower East Side came to be rented by black families.

The timing was fortuitous. The decade of mass migration from the rural South had just begun. Also on the move were blacks from the British West Indies (three hundred thousand would immigrate between 1900 and 1930, mostly to New York City). Other people of color came from Latin America, Haiti, the French West Indies, the Virgin Islands, and Africa itself. As this population, with its varied cultures, moved in, the whites moved out, often to largely rural sections of the Bronx that were being built up now that they were reachable on the very same Lenox Avenue line.

But it was no loss. Like New York, like America, Harlem too became multitongued and multicultural. It too now had the ingredients which inspire intellectual and artistic activity.

And so it was that giants like W. E. B. Dubois, Duke Ellington, Langston Hughes, and Zora Neale Hurston chose to live in Harlem— "warm, rambunctious, sassy Harlem," Hughes called it—where black political theorists and composers, black poets and novelists, black artists and photographers gathered to create as remarkable and enviable a cultural renaissance as America has ever known.

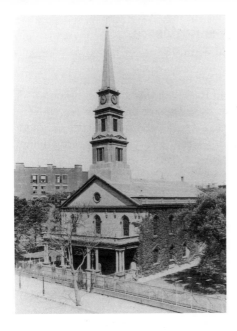

The present St. Mark's-in-the-Bowery, an Episcopal church, was built in 1799; the original, Peter Stuyvesant's Dutch Reform chapel on "the Bouwerie," was sited on the same land.

African Tour

1 St. Mark's-in-the-Bowery, East 10th Street at Second Avenue

In this churchyard lies the grave of Peter Stuyvesant, first governor of New Amsterdam. Stuyvesant, for all his distinction in New York history, was a tough, narrow-minded man. He wanted neither Jews nor Catholics nor most Protestants in the colony. Indeed, the only religious observances he permitted were those of the Dutch Reform Church. Records show, however, that forty African slaves and freemen worshiped here during the years of Dutch rule as members of the chapel Stuyvestant had built in his manor house on this site.

It is believed that servants, both blacks and white, were buried in a secondary plot belonging to the church, possibly at 12th Street between First and Second avenues.

2 | Isaac Hopper Residence, 110 Second Avenue

Thought to have been a waiting station of the Underground Railroad, this site was home to Isaac T. Hopper, a Quaker businessman, who was a vice-president of the railroad. He is credited with having written or aided in writing many slave narratives, including one by Solomon Northrup, a free black New Yorker who was kidnapped by bounty hunters and taken to Louisiana as a slave.

Northrup was not the only free black to be so treated. Kidnapping was so widespread in the City that in 1835 the Vigilance Committee of New York was formed to expose the kidnapping rings and to aid the victims. Hopper may or may not have been a member, but he is thought to have been instrumental in Northrup's return to his family in the North.

Among the main terminals of the railroad were the black churches in Manhattan, and black ministers were among the principal "conductors." (David Ruggles [see stop #8], also a vice-president of the railroad, was its only black officer.) Best known of all who were involved, however, was neither male nor minister. It was the heroic Harriet Tubman, the escaped slave who made at least nineteen forays into the South to rescue her fellow blacks and bring them north into freedom.

Then and now, Cooper Union massively dominates Astor Place, but when gaslights flickered down on the audiences who came to attend lectures in the Great Hall, a cutlery and glassware shop commercialized the western side of the building.

Frederick Douglass, whose powerfully abolitionist *North Star* was published out of Rochester, New York, escaped from slavery as a man of twenty-one. By the time he first spoke at Cooper Union, he was known around the world through his autobiography, the *Narrative of the Life of Frederick Douglass.*

3 | Cooper Union for the Advancement of Science and Art, Astor Place

This still lively, still tuition-free institution was established by the inventor and industrialist Peter Cooper in 1859, twelve years after the founding of the first of the City's tuition-free colleges, the Free Academy (later renamed the College of the City of New York and generally called CCNY).

As Cooper saw it, the schooling available at the Free Academy was insufficient for the needs of a young nation and for the working classes whose lot he hoped to improve. Judging from his own experience, he believed America needed technically educated artisans as much as or more than classically educated professionals.

Among the speakers in the Union's Great Hall were Abraham Lincoln (in 1860) and the great black abolitionist Frederick Douglass, who addressed audiences on subjects ranging from the future of blacks in the southern states to the Emancipation Proclamation and a Negro army. 11

Many of the black soldiers standing at attention here enlisted in the Union army at the urging of Frederick Douglass. The cheering crowd is celebrating the presentation of the colors to the members of the 20th U.S. Colored Infantry in March 1864, eight months after the Draft Riots.

4 | Washington Square Park

The first person to have cleared the land beneath the trees, playgrounds, and statues of the present-day park was Big Manuel, one of the slaves brought to the Dutch colony of New Netherlands in 1625. After nineteen years, he was freed to farm near this then-swampy ground.

At the end of the eighteenth century, the land was used as a potter's field; perhaps as many as twenty-two thousand bodies, many dead from yellow fever, lie beneath the present-day park. From 1826 to 1828 the Square served as a military parade ground and as the site of the City's scaffold. Shortly thereafter, it was gentrified into a park described by Henry James as the "ideal of quiet and genteel retirement." (If he knew of the episode, he chose to overlook the 1835 confrontation between the police and a band of stonemasons protesting the use of convict labor to erect New York University's earliest buildings.)

For James, who was born at 21 Washington Place, the Square held gentle memories. As he wrote in the novel that would later be dramatized as *The Heiress*, "It was here that you took your first walks abroad, following the nursery-maid with unequal step, and sniffing up the strange odor of the ailanthus trees which at that time formed the principal umbrage of the Square...."

The tender scene depicted by the novelist changed forever when the memorial arch, designed by architects Mead, McKim, and White, was completed in 1895. Buses—the double-deckers that once plied Fifth Avenue—reversed direction in the park, and James's implicit hush was soon broken by the sound of their exhaust. When the buses were banned, their noise was replaced by boom boxes, dog runs, and the thud of feet as students raced to classes at New York University.

5   St. Benedict the Moor, 210 Bleecker Street

The first Roman Catholic church for blacks north of the Mason-Dixon Line was established here in 1883. When an adjacent avenue was widened in 1927, the building was demolished and the congregation moved to West 53rd Street, in what was then a middle-class black neighborhood.

Black churches of all denominations satisfied much more than the religious aspirations of their congregations. As gathering centers for like-minded people, they gave impetus to the formation of benevolent associations, lending libraries, church schools, literary and musical societies, and lecture series with speakers on subjects ranging from history to science.

Catherine (Katy) Ferguson's identification for this picture is as the founder of modern Sunday schools in New York. But "modern" is misleading; her school was not religious in its orientation.

6 | Catherine Ferguson Residence, 74 Thompson Street

According to the federal census of 1830, seven black men who lived on Thompson Street owned seventeen female slaves. The women may or may not have been their wives and daughters; the census didn't say. In the 1850s, this address marked the last home of Catherine (Katy) Ferguson, a black pastry-shop owner believed to have served as foster mother to forty-eight children in the course of her life—twenty-eight black orphans and twenty white ones.

Ferguson was clearly a remarkable woman, not least because her dates are given in the *Encyclopedia of New York City* as ?1749-1854. What is not in doubt is her establishment in 1793 of the interracial School for the Poor, possibly at this very location, certainly on Thompson Street. An offshoot of the Sunday school movement that had evolved in England a few years earlier, her school provided instruction to children and adults alike.

No more than the original Sunday schools was her school religious; Sunday, as the sole day of rest, was the only day on which workers were free to attend.

7 | African Grove Theater, Bleecker and Grove Streets

From 1821 to 1829, this theater—whose location had earlier been a tea and ice cream garden for free blacks—offered black audiences free admission to such plays as Richard III and Othello. As a young man, the celebrated black actor Ira Aldridge (1807-1867) performed here.

White newspapers noted the existence of the theater as a curiosity but did not give the performances any serious critical attention. It has been said that the omission was the result of the papers' editors scoffing at the idea of Africans thinking they could perform Shakespeare. It is also possible that the editors thought their (overwhelmingly white) readers would not be interested in attending an African theater where, had they chosen to come, they would have been restricted to seats in the rear. Responding to discrimination in a city where Africans were generally excluded or made to sit in the rear, this first black theater in America wittily practiced reverse segregation.

Shown here as Othello, Ira Aldridge performed in many Shakespearean roles during a distinguished career on the stages of the British Isles and Europe. He died in Poland, a royally bemedaled British citizen.

8 David Ruggles Home, 36 Lispenard Street

For one year, 1838, this was the address of David Ruggles, "Father of the Underground Railroad." A one-time seaman, Ruggles owned and operated a grocery store. As a leader of the Vigilance Committee [see stop #2], he is credited with having helped more than six hundred slaves, including Frederick Douglass, escape to freedom via the railroad. Ruggles's activism also led him to print and edit the nation's first black magazine, *Mirror of Liberty*, and to establish at 67 Lispenard Street an African-American bookstore, as well as a reading room and circulating library. The latter enterprise survived for only a year. Presumably its popularity with blacks and abolitionists incited a mob to destroy it.

9 African Burial Ground Excavation Site, Duane Street and Broadway

Now the best-known archeological site in the City, saved when black activists brought a federal building project to a halt in 1991, this six-acre plot is thought to have held the remains of as many as twenty thousand black men, women, and children who lived, and died, in colonial New York.

The cemetery, which lay outside the City proper, beyond a wall that once stretched from river to river along what is now Chambers Street, was also the final resting place for Indians (they too were held as slaves), paupers, and military prisoners.

Because the colonists feared that any large gathering of their African slaves might produce a revolt, they limited to twelve the number permitted to congregate, even at a burial.

When the cemetery was closed in the 1790s—after perhaps a hundred years of use—a new burial ground for blacks was opened on Chrystie Street, and the identifiable bodies from this site were disinterred and reburied. Like the Negro Cemetery on Church Street, on land which was part of Trinity Parish, it is no longer extant. But then neither are dozens of graveyards established by white congregations. In the three and a half centuries since Manhattan was settled by the white man, not just cemeteries but also hills, forests, and farms have all disappeared, banished by New York's passion to cram more and more people into its tight little island.

10 Colored Reform Church of the Dutch, Duane and Hudson Streets

This church operated out of a schoolroom—possibly in the African Free School #5—from 1826 to sometime before 1850. The congregation may well have included members descended from the slaves of New Amsterdam, some of whom were known to have been married in the Dutch Reform ritual. Indeed, between 1624 and 1664, 28 percent of all marriages in the City's Dutch Reform churches involved Africans.

11 | Mother Zion African Church, 158 Church Street

Increasingly dissatisfied with segregated pews in white churches, James Varick and Peter Williams, supported by other black leaders, established the original A(frican) M(ethodist) E(piscopal) Zion church—Mother Zion—in 1799; it became independent in 1801. Although free blacks were congregants of Dutch Reform, Baptist, and Episcopalian churches, Methodism, because of its stand on abolition, was the religion particularly favored by the blacks of the City.

Varick was a well-to-do shoemaker with a shop on Orange (now Baxter) Street. Because the Methodist church he attended segregated his people, he first organized separate all-black meetings above a cabinetmaker's shop. That was in 1796. Three years later, he was leading the African Methodist Episcopal Zion Church. He was followed by Peter Williams.

Unlike Varick, who was presumably born free, Peter Williams was born a slave and converted to Methodism. He worked as sexton of the City's first Methodist Episcopal church, the Wesley Chapel, at 44 John Street. The white trustees of the chapel had purchased him from a Loyalist for the sum of forty dollars "to protect the sexton from the indignities of the auction block." Like other founders of Mother Zion, Williams retained his membership in the Wesley Chapel even after Mother Zion was established.

The independent black churches were (and are) vastly important. Beyond the roles they and their leaders played in the Underground Railroad and in working for abolition, the churches—along with self-help organizations [see stop #17] and the Free Schools [see stop #15]—served to unify the blacks. Equally important, they demonstrated that there was no lack of strength and solidarity in the black community. No white philanthropists were required to provide direction.

The front page of this March 1827 issue of *Freedom's Journal,* with its motto, "Righteousness Exalteth a Nation," carries not the news of the week but matter far more important—accounts of the black experience.

12 | ## Freedom's Journal,
150-52 Church Street

Freedom's Journal, a weekly newspaper edited by John Russwurm and the Reverend Samuel Cornish, was published at this location from 1827 to 1829. It was established by a group of black leaders—Peter Williams [see stop #11] among them—and its startup costs were funded by a joint stock company they organized.

The *Journal* circulated widely, not only through cities in the North but also as far abroad as Port-au-Prince, Haiti, and Liverpool, England. It was the first of more than thirty-five black-published and -edited newspapers that would originate in New York State during the nineteenth century. In the City, pre-Civil War newspapers run by and for blacks included the *Weekly Advocate,* with offices at 2 Frankfort Street; Cornish's own *The Rights of All* (the renamed *Freedom's Journal*); and *The Colored American,* which he published from 9 Spruce Street.

In the *Journal,* Russwurm and Cornish dedicated themselves to abolishing slavery and overturning the legal restrictions still handicapping free persons of color. "We wish to plead our own cause," they wrote in their first editorial; "too long have others spoke for us...." But in fact, Russwurm and Cornish had separate causes and could not always speak with one voice. They split over the question of colonization.

19

12

cont.

The American Colonization Society, established in Washington, D.C., largely by southern slave-holders, promoted the idea that free blacks should return to Africa. To that end the Society raised money privately, and received some from the U.S. Congress, to purchase land in what is now Liberia. Were the donations signs of repentance for holding a people in slavery? Or should we draw less benign implications: that the only blacks wanted in the United States were slaves and servants, and that free blacks represented a dangerous element in American society?

Whichever the case, Russwurm needed no prompting from the Colonization Society. As a recipient of one of the first degrees earned by a black man in America (from Bowdoin College in 1826), he came to the conclusion that people of his race would always be viewed as inferior in the United States. He not only urged his black sisters and brothers to return to Africa—about twelve thousand did—he went himself, emigrating to Liberia in 1829 to take a position in its department of education.

Cornish, on the other hand, a graduate of Princeton Theological Seminary and leader of the Coloured Presbyterian Church on Rose Street, became a leader of the Negro Convention of Free People of Color, formed to protest against the Colonization Society. At the Convention's first meeting, held in Philadelphia in 1830, Cornish and other black leaders of the day—ministers and businessmen (including Thomas Downing [stop #14]) who attended in order to represent the concerns of the under-privileged as well as those of the middle class—made it clear that their people had played, and were still playing, a significant role in the making of the nation. They refused to leave a country they saw as their own, their native land. As they put it:

We rejoice that we are thrown into a revolution where the contest is not for land territory, but for freedom; theweapons are not carnal, but spiritual; where the struggle is not for blood, but for right; and where the bow is for the power of God, and the arrow the instrument of divine justice.

Mary Church Terrell at the height of her fame as an advocate for the rights of women.

13 National Association of Colored Women, 9 Murray Street

Founded in 1896, this federation of two hundred women's clubs stressed the equality of women and, in support of its self-improvement program, ran employment agencies. Among its members was the wife of Booker T. Washington of Tuskeegee Institute. But its best-known member was its leader, Mary Church Terrell, a militant feminist and lecturer on the rights of women, who was also enrolled as the first black member of the Association of College Women.

Downing's Oyster House was most likely the building on left closest to Federal Hall. Corner sites were preferred for eateries that sold alcohol because, in defiance of Sunday closing laws, customers—policemen among them—could sneak in for a drink through the side door leading to the proprietor's living quarters.

14 | Downing's Oyster House, 5 Broad Street

For some thirty years, Thomas Downing (after whom Downing Street may have been named) was a well-to-do restaurateur whose oyster house at this location was much favored by politicians and businessmen. (Oyster selling was a trade pursued by many free blacks, perhaps because the mariners among them knew the location of the most accessible beds.) Story has it that in 1835, casks of vinegar and wine from Downing's restaurant were poured out in an attempt to quench a notable fire that crisped much of Wall Street and its environs. Not that it did much good. The veteran tour guide Joyce Gold relates that 674 buildings, on twenty acres of downtown land, were destroyed that cold December.

Downing was, however, more than a successful restaurateur. He was a person who carried weight in the community, someone powerful enough to help discharge the white man who headed the African Free Schools [see stop #15].

His son, George T. Downing, also ran restaurants, one at 690 Broadway and another in Rhode Island. The younger Downing, a graduate of the African Free Schools, would also organize black labor, become vice-president of the National Negro Labor Movement, and, in 1859, chairman of the National Convention of Colored Men, founded in Philadelphia.

15

African Dorcas Society/African Free Schools, 245 Williams Street

The African Dorcas Society, the earliest organization for black women in the City, was founded in 1828 at the urging of Peter Williams, John Russwurm, and other leaders of the black community. Composed of women, some of whom were the wives of prominent black businessmen, the Society solicited material, old clothes, and money to buy shoes for youngsters who otherwise would have been unable to attend the African Free Schools, one branch of which—for girls—may have been located at this site.

Meeting twice a month to mend and sew for the students, the Dorcas Society women formed another of the self-help organizations in the community.

The first of the African Free Schools was opened in 1787 by white abolitionists (among them Alexander Hamilton, John Jay, and Daniel Tompkins, governor of the state and later James Monroe's vice-president) belonging to the New York Manumission Society.

The schools—which provided educational and vocational training—were numbered, just as, later, the public schools would be. Over time, the individual schools would move from one location to another, following the movement of the black population. The addresses of the first schools are up for debate; the addresses of the later schools seem to be firm:

The Wall Street area after the Great Fire of December 1835.

15

cont.

#1. 245 Williams Street; 51 Laurens Street

#2. 135 (girls) and 137 (boys) Mulberry Street

#3. "Sixth Avenue"; 120 Amity Street (boys/girls); 15th Street and Seventh Avenue; "Yorkville"

#4. 135 Mulberry Street; 125 Rivington Street; 117th Street near 2nd Avenue

#5. 161 Duane Street; 19 Thomas Street

#6. 108 Columbia Street; 125 Rivington Street; 1167 Broadway

#7. 38 White Street

The first students—forty males, the children of slaves and former slaves—ranged in age from six to sixteen. In addition to the standard primary school subjects—reading, writing, arithmetic ("cyphering"), geography, speech, penmanship, and grammar—there were also vocational studies: navigation and astronomy to prepare them for the vocation of seaman. Female students, who were enrolled at least by 1791, studied needlework and dressmaking under a woman. Both sexes also received instruction in morals and good manners.

There is some evidence that, at the start, for parents who could pay, tuition was a dollar per quarter; needy students were admitted without charge.

At the beginning there was grave opposition to the schools, but little by little acceptance grew, especially when, in 1810, New York slave masters were required to teach all slave children to read Scripture. By 1823 enrollment had reached a peak of eight hundred students, in attendance from from 8 A.M. to 5 P.M. on weekdays and until noon on Saturdays. After that date, enrollment began to fall—in part because the black population was moving elsewhere in the City, in part because, as Russwurm wrote, "students and parents were no longer content to rely upon a white man for their education."

The New York African Free School

ERECTED IN THE YEAR 1815.

By the

New York Society for promoting the Manumission of Slaves.

Officers of the Society.

Cadwallader D. Colden President.

Valentine Seamans Vice Presdt. George Newbold 2d Vice Pres.

John Murray Jun Treasurer.

Samuel Simpson Secrety. Samuel Lushton Asst. Secrety.

Trustees of the School.

John Murray Jun Chairman. Thomas Collins Secry.

B. I. Collins Robert C. Cornell. J. T. Johnson.

Peter Jay. W. Pott Somers. Samuel Parsons.

Thomas Leland. W. Van Wagenen. George T. Mott.

Samuel Wood.

Teacher.

Charles C. Andrews.

That only one teacher is named for this substantial school demonstrates that it was run under the Lancastrian system: one teacher, many monitors.

The white man—one Charles Andrews, the principal instructor and someone who supported the colonization movement [see stop #12]—was forced to resign by Downing and a few like-minded activists. He was replaced by a black teacher who also followed the Lancaster method, devised in England to handle huge classes at the lowest possible cost. In this monitorial system, also employed in white schools, older students—boys and girls thirteen and fourteen years old—worked as apprentice teachers. It was they who taught, for a pittance, under the very limited direction of one or more "professionals."

With the shift of control from white philanthropists to concerned members of the black community, enrollment grew again: a total of 1,068 in schools #1 through #4 in 1832. In the middle of that year, two new schools had to be opened: #5 and #6. All now had black teachers.

The schools came under the control of the state-chartered Public School Society in the 1830s and the newly formed Board of Education in 1842, but they remained segregated until 1873.

15

cont.

The following year, the legislature required the City's public colleges—CCNY and the Normal (later Hunter College)—to admit all black students who met the qualifications.

From grammar school straight into college? Yes. Although boastfully in the vanguard in most matters, New York City was retrograde when it came to high school education. For the vast majority of young people, black and white alike, those who completed grammar school went directly out to work. If they desired further education, they studied at night in advanced classes taught by the principals and assistant principals of a few exceptional schools. Eventually, an Evening High School—for males only—was provided for the academically ambitious. (The well-to-do had private academies or tutors to prepare them for colleges considered more prestigious than CCNY and the Normal.) For other studious young people—those whose families were not snobbish and did not require their earnings—there were the two City-supported colleges, where the courses taught during the first year of study were essentially preparatory—at the high school level.

When finally, in 1897, the City established its first day high schools, it became the last major city in the United States to do so.

16

St. Philip's Church, Centre Street

St. Philip's, an Episcopal church founded in 1810 for black congregants, by some accounts had three different locations on Centre Street: #31, #24, and #84, and one on Mulberry Street, and that its second location—replacing the first, which burned—was led by Peter Williams, Jr., son of the pastor of Mother Zion [see stop #11], a graduate of the African Free Schools and an ardent opponent of slavery.

On the other hand, *Early New York Houses* by William Pelletrean records that St. Phillip's [sic] "received lots for church building June 25th, 1818, on Mulberry St. The view presented [see illustration] shows the entire front between Leonard and Duane Streets. This church replaces the first church which burned in 1819, the new building was erected soon after."

It is difficult to ascertain the truth of matters that date so far back in City history. But it is certainly reasonable to assume that the families that would form the earliest congregation of St. Philip's initially came together in modest surroundings—not in a church building but in a room in someone's home or shop, most likely on Centre Street. What we can be sure of is that by 1818 the congregation was sufficiently large and established to "receive lots for church building" on Mulberry Street.

A hundred years after its founding, St Philip's moved to 214 West 134th Street; and it was from its Harlem pulpit in 1989 that a black woman, the Right Rev. Barbara Harris of Massachusetts, the first of her sex to be elected a bishop in the Episcopal Church, gave her first sermon in the New York diocese.

This impressive building at 81-83 Mulberry Street, shown as it looked c. 1840, was most likely the fifth location of the congregation of St. Philip's Church. Less certain is which body of worshippers was led by Peter Williams, Jr., the one that met here or the one that met at 24 Centre Street.

17 New York African Society for Mutual Relief, 42 Baxter Street

Established in 1809 with a charter membership that included James Varick [see stop #11] and Peter Williams, Jr. [see stop #16], the Society provided sickness and death insurance for its members. When the building was demolished, it was discovered that the Society had also used its premises to operate a waiting station of the Underground Railroad.

Although it resembled the mutual-aid societies that would be formed by Germans, Irish, Chinese, Jews, and Italians on the Lower East Side, the African Society for Mutual Relief also differed from them. According to Elizabeth Grossi, a contemporary scholar, the Society stressed the importance of hard work and business success. Prospering businesses, it was hoped, would have advantages above and beyond the personal. By demonstrating that blacks could "do" for themselves, their success would help to reduce racism and to undermine paternalistic arguments supporting slavery.

18 Old St. Patrick's Cathedral, 263 Mulberry Street

The first African-American candidate for canonization, the Haitian-born Pierre Toussaint (1766-1853), was once the most fashionable hairdresser in the City. He was buried in a tomb still extant in this churchyard, although he and his family worshiped at St. Peter's Catholic Church on Barclay Street [see Irish stop #1]. His remains, however, are no longer here; they were removed and reinterred at St. Patrick's Cathedral on Fifth Avenue.

Today, because his canonization is being promoted, Toussaint has become a controversial figure. On one side, his loyalty to his owners, his choice to accompany them to New York and remain a slave instead of joining the slave rebellion in Haiti, his raising of money for a white orphanage—such behavior has led some people, both black and white, to label him an Uncle Tom. On the other side, his goodness and piety—he nursed cholera patients; he opened his home to black orphans; he attended Mass at St. Peter's daily for sixty-six years; he bought the freedom of several slaves—led others to view Toussaint as a true hero, like the once-beloved character in Harriet Beecher Stowe's antislavery novel, *Uncle Tom's Cabin.*

Whatever side one comes down on, the fact remains that Toussaint—freed at the age of forty-five, when his widowed mistress died—was greatly admired by New York society women who paid him astonishing sums to coif their hair, sums which he invariably put to charitable uses.

Perhaps more politically conscious than given credit for, Pierre Toussaint not only tendered charity to poor blacks and whites but also gave shelter to political refugees from Haiti and France.

EPILOGUE

Few African Americans live on the Lower East Side today. For those who remain in Manhattan, a widely expanded Harlem is their primary home—the slums of Harlem for too many, the gentrified neighborhoods of Harlem for too few. Numbers of black and interracial families also live on Roosevelt Island, perhaps the most integrated community of the City. But unlike the other groups whose first American settlements were on the Lower East Side, the majority of African Americans are still confined to segregated neighborhoods, no matter what their professional accomplishments, no matter where in the outer boroughs, nearby counties, or the United States at large they have chosen to live.

Six Tours of the **Lower East Side**

E. 12TH

E. 11TH

E. 10TH

12

11

E. 9TH

ST. MARK'S PLACE

10

13

TOMPKINS
SQUARE
PARK

SECOND AVE

E. 7TH

FIRST AVE

AVENUE A

E. 4TH

9

BOWERY

E. 3RD

ND **8**

HOUSTON

7

14

S

S

STANTON

M9, 21
B 39

15

CHRYSTIE

FORSYTH

ELDRIDGE

ALLEN

ORCHARD

LUDLOW

ESSEX

NORFOLK

RIVINGTON

3

DELANCEY

S

S

5

MULBERRY

MOTT

ELIZABETH

4

BROOME

2

6

1 GRAND

S

B, D, Q
M103

HESTER

German Heritage

Prior to the massive influx of Eastern
European Jews after 1880, the Lower East Side
housed more German speakers than most cities
in Germany. So evident was the German presence that the 10th, 11th, 13th, and 17th wards
came to be called Kleindeutschland—Little
Germany. (A similar label was to be attached to
Washington Heights in the 1930s. Refuge to
thousands of German Jews fleeing Hitler, the
area was nicknamed the Fourth Reich. Today
Washington Heights is home to immigrants
from the Dominican Republic.)

Germans had been on board the first ships
bringing Europeans to New Amsterdam. So
little did they stand out in the small Dutch
colony that a young man born in Wesel served
as director general of the Dutch West India
Company. Legend has it that this chap—his
name was Peter Minuit (or Minnewit)—purchased Manhattan Island from the Indians for
twenty-four gold dollars, or for trinkets worth
that sum.

Equally skilled in the fine art of the deal was
John (originally Johann) Jacob Astor, an immigrant living with his family in a small German
community south of City Hall in the early
1800s. Born the son of a butcher in Waldorf, a
village in southwestern Germany, Astor came
to New York in 1784 at the age of twenty, his

In the United States today, more people are descended from Germans than from any other immigrant group. Embarking from Hamburg are, judging from their clothes, a full economic range of some of our ancestors.

only capital a few musical instruments he had brought with him. Starting out apprenticed to a furrier, he was soon traveling upstate and into Canada in order to buy pelts. By the turn of the century, he had extended his reach as far as China and was worth a quarter of a million dollars.

Although originating in furs, Astor's fortune—which grew to be the largest in America—soared as his commercial interests expanded. In his later years, he concentrated heavily on real estate. Story has it that he once sold a piece of land on Wall Street for $8,000. When the buyer remarked on the exceptionally good deal he'd received, Astor replied, "With those $8,000 I will buy eighty plots north of Canal Street, and when your plot is worth $12,000, mine will be worth $80,000."

He did not exaggerate. The area north of Canal Street, toward the East River, became the premier building site for tenements when immigrants newer than Astor sought immediate and cheap housing. So this immigrant, whose impressive collection of rare books would, after his death, form one of the sources of the New York Public Library, also flourished as one of the City's early landlords.

Although Germans began arriving in number around 1817 and again in 1832, their largest wave of immigration followed the Revolutions of 1848. Some came surreptitiously; some came with official permission of the government—a permission that required payment of all outstanding debts by the prospective traveler. But when hunger and unemployment in the German states increased the demand for public assistance, local governments were often only too happy to offer incentives to those willing to leave. In 1855, for example, a full third of the fifteen hundred inhabitants of the village of Winzeln on the Neckar consented to emigrate. The needy among them received a hundred gulden each to hasten their going.

Besides those Winzelnites who left voluntarily —if not necessarily gladly—and those who welcomed the financial incentive, there were those forced to emigrate by court decree. These were the "undesirables"—people with criminal records and people on public assistance. One of the latter was a thirty-seven-year-old unwed mother of five children. She was deported. Her five children, however, were "allowed" to remain; under state guardianship, they were "to complete their education," which was often nothing more than a form of forced labor.

P rior to the 1850s, the sailing ships on which the immigrants came to America took anywhere from ten to twenty-four weeks for the journey. Later, faster ships, still under sail but fitted with engines and paddle wheels, could make the trip in six weeks. In all cases, conditions were frightful. "You can recognize an emigrants' ship by the stench."

Once propeller-driven steamships began to ply the Atlantic, and with them some governmental supervision over sanitation, the length of the voyage from Bremen to New York took a mere seventeen days. Still, fresh food lasted only so long. All too soon the diet of steerage passengers became potatoes, herring, and dirty water.

The immigrants came from all the German-speaking states and provinces, but those emigrating after the 1848 Revolutions came primarily from the southwest—from Baden, Württemberg, and the Palatinate. Those arriving later in the century came from the northern states—Prussia, Saxony, and Hannover. Some, as already noted, came because they were driven from their homeland. Others—Protestants, Catholics, and Jews alike—came to seek political and religious freedom, or to find adventure, prosperity, or both. Still others came because disastrous harvests and mortgaged farms left them no alternative.

Those intending to settle elsewhere in the new country usually arrived in family groups. Those who chose New York City were mostly single men and women. Not only were potential spouses available, but German servants were in demand in the households of well-to-do Americans. Among the many help-wanted ads in the *New-Yorker Staats-Zeitung* of April 1, 1870, were notices that translated as: "Girl to

The German grocer—plump and mustached, according to the stereotype—and his customers. In the rear is a wine and liquor shop, situated, as usual, on a corner where the location allowed patrons, ostensibly obeying the law, to enter through the owner's living quarters on Sundays when the bars were shut.

clean, $7 per week. Sundays free"; "Healthy, respectable nursemaid, $30 per mo."; and "Nice young girl, must speak English, general housework, small family, $5-6 per month."

Within Kleindeutschland, all kinds of German accents could be heard. But the accents didn't mix. Like associated with like. There were almost as few marriages between Prussians and Bavarians as there were between Germans and Irish. Even those occupations monopolized by Germans—piano and cigar making, orchestral performance, carpentry, shopkeeping—were divided according to areas of origin. Before the 1860s, the grocer, for example, almost invariably came from Hannover or Hamburg.

Another occupation frequently held was that of saloonkeeper. And although the work did not automatically lead to Tammany Hall, as it did for the Irish [see Irish stop #16], there was no denying German political power. When Republican Theodore Roosevelt, as police commissioner, determined to enforce a Sunday closing of bars—an action so wildly unpopular that the editor of the *Staats-Zeitung* [see stop #12] accused him of prejudice—the Germans, normally of Roosevelt's party, turned 80 percent of their 1895 vote over to the Democrats.

Kleindeutschland may sound narrow, provincial. It was not. To be sure, it was self-contained. Residents bought from German-owned stores, attended German theaters, listened to German music, visited German doctors in German clinics, took their amusements in German saloons and *Biergärten*. Above all, they joined German clubs—*Vereine*—that were the distinguishing feature of Kleindeutschland's social and political life.

But provincial? Not altogether. Where the outside world did not directly impinge—schools, policemen—it was expected to stand inspection. The Cafe Europa (on Division Street) and the Cafe International (on Chatham Square), for example, both of which advertised in the daily German-language papers, subscribed for their patrons to *two hundred* French, German, and English newspapers and journals.

LORD & TAYLOR,

Importers and Wholesale and Retail Dealers in

DRY GOODS.

Nos. 255, 257, 259 & 261 Grand Street, cor. Chrystie, N. Y.

If each numbered address spanned the City's regulation twenty-five-foot lot, Lord & Taylor's frontage covered at least a hundred feet of Grand Street.

German Tour

1 Grand Street

Grand Street was once truly grand. In the mid-nineteenth century it was the major thoroughfare and shopping center of the Lower East Side. Lord & Taylor sold dry goods in a shop at the corner of Chrystie Street. The Seligman brothers, future bankers, ran a hat and cap store between Pitt and Ridge streets. Halm's Cigar Store, which doubled as a lending library, boasted four thousand volumes on its shelves. The Harmonie Club, long since settled in a McKim, Mead & White edifice on East 60th Street, had its first location, complete with library and reading room, just off Grand on Ludlow Street. Off Grand at Orchard Street stood the first *Turnverein Halle*.

The original Temple Emanu-El, located today on Fifth Avenue and 65th Street, held its first services in a rented room on the second floor of a

37

1

cont.

private house at #202 1/2, near Clinton Street. The congregation, composed of thirty-three families, then moved its services to 56 Chrystie Street (now a parking lot), and continued to move in a generally northern direction as its membership grew more prosperous and could afford not merely to purchase but to build its own temple.

Oddly enough, Emanu-El did not begin as a religious institution. Its earliest members had joined together initially to participate in a literary society. With secular culture on their lips, their adoption of Reform Judaism—Emanu-El was the first such congregation in the City—was a natural and reasonable progression [see also stop #15].

2

Socialreformer Halle, 281 Grand Street

The Social Reform Association, which defined itself as a cultural as much as a political entity, was founded in 1845 by a group of German exiles under the leadership of Hermann Kriege, whom both Marx and Engels spurned because his association affiliated itself with American Democrats concerned with the nonproletarian issue of land—land for settlers.

The *Halle* remained on Grand Street throughout the 1860s, and although it continued to be a center for trade union activity and made space available to politically minded enterprises like Gustav and Amalie Struve's short-lived newspaper, *Soziale Republik*, its own political force waned. As time passed, more and more of its members joined principally to enjoy singing societies, lectures, theatricals, sporting events, parades, picnics, and, yes, drinking. Fun and games with one's *Landsleute* held enormous attraction for the German immigrant in America.

3 Freie Schule (Free School), 171 Chrystie Street

The newspaper-publishing Struves [see stop #2] argued in editorials that their *Freie Schule* was, and must be, founded on science—science, not religion, not the Bible. And many veterans of the Revolutions of 1848 agreed. More particularly, they believed that their children deserved an education based on real—that is, German—cultural traditions [see stop #9]. Thus, during the 1850s, German schools proliferated on the Lower East Side, although sometimes less for the sake of students than to provide income for the semi-intellectual ex-revolutionaries who preferred teaching to joining the ranks of the industrial proletariat.

Some schools taught their students entirely in German (this was a subject of controversy in the German community), some were bilingual (this too was controversial), and more than a few offered religious instruction (not so much controversial as anathema to some, essential to others). Most of the schools charged tuition. "Free" at the Struves' school meant free-thinking at a cost of twenty cents per child per week, or thirty-seven cents for two children, or fifty cents for three. These prices, the Struves argued, were affordable: only a quarter of the tuition at a more fashionable *Schule* on Market Street.

In the white building below the Fletcher's Castoria advertisement lies Sinsheimer's, the Essex Street saloon where B'nai B'rith was born.

4 Odd Fellows Hall, 98 Forsyth Street

A favorite meeting place for the lodges, clubs, associations, and other *Vereine* in Klein-deutschland was the Odd Fellows Hall on Forsyth Street. (Several others halls belonging to the Odd Fellows existed in the area, including one on Grand Street.)

Probably in imitation (or envy) of the Masons, the German Union, first of the German lodges in New York, was founded in 1819. The ensuing fad among Germans for secret societies lasted well past the middle of the nineteenth century. The Odd Fellows, the Pythagoras, the Deutsche Orden der Harugari, the Hermannssöhne, the Druiden—whatever their names, they saw themselves as guardians of German culture in a culturally barren, and not infrequently hostile, American world.

Their mottoes bespoke idealism—*Freundschaft, Liebe, Humanität* (Friendship, Love, Humanity) or *Glaube, Liebe, Hoffnung* (Faith, Love, Hope)—but the coming together in lodges also had a practical purpose: to establish mutual benefit societies which extended philanthropy to their particular communities.

One of the earliest and most vigorous of the lodges, the Independent Order of B'nai B'rith (Sons of the Covenant), was founded in 1843 in Sinsheimer's beer parlor on Essex Street and later moved to a location of its own: Covenant Hall at 56 Orchard Street. The order was established in part because the Masons—the most significant of all fraternal lodges, international in membership and holding to ideals such as fellowship and religious toleration—did not admit Jews. In turn, B'nai B'rith initially closed its doors, but not its philanthropic interests, to their coreligionists from Eastern Europe. For them, the members offered Americanization programs and an employment agency that sought to find them jobs—jobs away from New York.

Not many decades after its founding, B'nai B'rith also went international. The Vienna lodge, established in 1895, had Sigmund Freud as a member.

5 Tenth Ward Hotel, Broome and Forsyth Streets

The first generation of German revolutionaries to arrive in New York came following the Revolutions of 1848. The second generation arrived after 1865; for them the Tenth Ward Hotel was a refuge and hub of activity. (Many decades later, in order to squeeze light and air into the area, the hotel's site and neighboring blocks stretching from Canal to Houston streets were turned into a strip of greensward named for Franklin D. Roosevelt's patrician mother.)

The young Samuel Gompers, founding father of the American Federation of Labor, received his first theoretical-political education at this hotel. The International Workingmen's Association (the "First International"), umbrella organization for various radical and socialist groups, was headquartered here from 1872 to 1876. The leader of its executive committee, Karl Marx himself, when faced with a split in the ranks,

5

cont.

recommended that the International relocate to New York, believing that socialist crosswinds would be less strong here than they were in London. (They were not.)

Education was one of the issues that greatly stirred the radical groups that congregated at the Tenth Ward Hotel. The older men, the veterans of '48, stood for free education for all; it was, they argued, a step on the road to liberation. The younger men, hard-nosed radicals, considered that position nothing more than bourgeois illusion. At least one '48er agreed: Friedrich Adolph Sorge, "adjutant for the great Karl" and forceful spokesman for the First International in New York, would have none of the free-education nonsense. "Liberation of the workers…is not at all dependent on public education…consciousness of their place in society [i.e., as members of the proletariat] is completely sufficient."

Before the Bowery became disreputable, it held such astonishingly lavish structures as the German Winter-Garden, where well-to-do immigrants in all their finery disported themselves like the "uptown" gentry they, or more likely their children, would eventually join.

6   The Bowery

Before the advent of the Great White Way—Times Square and environs—and the building of the Third Avenue El (completed in 1878), the Bowery was New York's premier amusement district. Once an Indian trail and later called by the Dutch "the road to [Peter Stuyvesant's] farm (bouwerij)," the Bowery during its German period was lined with theaters, bars, restaurants, cafes, banks, and stores (Hammacher Hardware, the original of Hammacher Schlemmer, had its shop at #209).

Possibly less prosperous than the patrons of the Winter-Garden, these Germans, with their children, imbibe beer at what may be the Atlantic Garden across the street. The musicians at the upper left play German tunes while the man who travels with his dog sketches a customer.

Although Avenue B was the place to go for purely German amusement, the Bowery held more than its share of ethnic gaiety. The German Winter-Garden and, across the street, the Atlantic Garden (#45 and #50, respectively) were among the largest and most elaborate of the *biergartens*. The Thalia, at #46, built in 1826 and originally christened The Bowery Theater, survived until the beginning of the twentieth century.

6

cont.

One after the other, the Stadttheater, the Deutsche Volksgarten, Lindenmuller's Odeon, the Deutsche Theater, and Baer & Michaelis's Odeon Vaudeville stretched north to Astor Place.

It was a *gemütliche* world. Entire families visted the *Biergärten* and, seated in the dress circles and first balconies of theaters, enjoyed the offerings on stage. No doubt they also went as families to the operas performed at the German Opera House and at the Stadttheater, which held the American premiere of Wagner's *Tannhäuser* in 1859. It was, after all, essential that the children receive regular doses of German culture. (Opera was largely in the hands of Italians, to such an extent that German opera was not infrequently premiered in the Italian language, but that hardly lessened the overwhelming presence of Germans in orchestras and on conductors' podiums.)

But despite the family atmosphere at its *Biergärten*, the Bowery was already tainted with the seediness that was eventually to envelop it. There were houses of prostitution offering "friendly service." There was the up-to-no-good Bismarck Hall at the corner of Pearl and Chatham streets, notorious for its series of cave-like chambers under the sidewalk. One can guess what the good burghers imagined took place in them. Was it they who whispered—*frisson* of horror—that the Grand Duke Alexei of Russia visited the place when in New York in the 1870s? While drinking and carousing in his Romanov way, he is supposed to have recognized one of the waitresses—none other than a Russian countess who had fallen into misfortune. Like the titled stranger in a contemporary romance, he thereupon bought her freedom.

7 Germania Assembly Rooms, The Bowery and Houston Street

On the northeast corner of this intersection stands a dilapidated two-story warehouse. In its good days it was the Germania (initally Steuben House). It contained a barroom, a restaurant, a billiards room, meeting rooms, and—still extant in the basement—a bowling alley. Beer flowed freely and food was appropriately priced; lunch, the main meal for Germans, could be had for fifteen cents.

Like the Tenth Ward Hotel and Odd Fellows Hall, the Germania was a place where local organizations held their meetings. It was here that the *Allgemeine Arbeiterfest* (General Workers' Festival) held the previews for its yearly gala. The 1871 program featured music—*An der Schönen Blauen Donau* ("The Beautiful Blue Danube")—recitals, tableaux-vivant, speeches of course, and the premiere of a local dissident's one-act play. Possibly fed to the teeth with the abstractions and arguments of both generations of radicals, he called his play *Kapital und Arbeit —eine Farce* ("Capital and Labor—a Farce").

The Dry Dock Savings Bank on the Bowery at Third Street around 1875, when banks dramatized their dependability through the fortresslike magnificence of their architecture. It was founded by "gentlemen" who claimed "to encourage thrift and prudence"—their own profits were not mentioned. Dry Dock's initial depositors were shipbuilders.

8 | Bowerie Lane Theater, 330 Bowery

Built for the Bond Street Savings Bank in 1874 by Henry Engelbert, a German architect, this cast-iron building replaced a less decorative structure built for the German Exchange Bank, which moved to #335 and is no more.

Many banking institutions served the German population. In addition to the German Exchange, there were the Deutsche Sparbank (Savings Bank) on 14th Street and Fourth Avenue, the Germania Bank at 215 Bowery, the New Amsterdam Savings Bank on the Bowery at Third Street, the still-remembered Dry Dock Savings Bank (originally at the foot of 10th Street, later on the Bowery), and, most notably, the long-lived Bowery Savings Bank, which was a presence in the City until its recent absorption by the Home Savings Bank.

Bowery Savings is said to be the first bank on the Lower East Side intentionally founded to serve the local population and to encourage thrift and industriousness. It opened with five depositors, who passed their money across a (borrowed) counter in the Butcher and Drover Bank at #124. Within the first year, 531 depositors had brought in $72,742. By 1873, its deposits amounted to $27 million. By 1894 it had moved into the now landmarked structure built by McKim, Mead & White at #130. (Its final headquarters, at 110 East 42nd Street, is another architectural treasure.)

The bank deserved its success. When it began to do especially well, its then president, in an effort to protect smaller clients, initiated a stipulation "that the interest on deposits exceeding one thousand dollars shall be at least one percent less than the interest allowed the others." Note here not only the high principles but also the sum of money dividing smaller depositors from larger ones. (Not that a thousand dollars wasn't serious money. Following the Civil War, a skilled worker earned about six hundred dollars in a year of full employment.)

But for their apparel, these Turners could be contemporaries. Workouts were serious business, demanding space, equipment, and (see the bearded man in a suit) a trainer to oversee the exercises.

9 | **Neue Turnhalle,
66-68 Fourth Street**

Today the Annex of La Mama, where Elaine
Stewart runs her brilliant avant-garde theater,
this last home of the *Turnhalle* looks pretty
much as it did when the Germans left it. Only
the two *Lokale* (bar/restaurants) to the right and
left of the main entrance have disappeared.

Founded in 1850 by a group of veterans of the
1848-49 unprisings, the *Turnverein*—the
"Sozialistischer Turnverein" as it was called in
those early years—not only furthered the classical idea of "a healthy mind in a healthy body"
but also the then very modern concept of "liberty,
prosperity, and free education for all."

Identified with progressive political movements
that demanded a nation-state and a constitution
—both radical departures from the tiny duke-
doms and principalities that composed most of
the German-speaking lands—the Turners (literally
"gymnasts") had become anathema to the
powers-that-were in the early nineteenth
century. After the defeat of the progressives in
the Revolutions of 1848, many Turners emigrated to the United States, where they tried to keep
alive the ideas that had shaken Europe. Some,
indeed, espoused atheism and socialism.

At the outset in New York, they met together in
temporary spaces, like the back rooms of bars
and hotels. One morning they found that their
current landlord had thrown out their equipment—parallel bars, weights, fencing sabers,
and the rest—all in a jumble on the street. They
then settled at 27-33 Orchard Street, a former
Quaker meeting house on the block between
Hester and Canal, and were able to purchase the
building before the decade was out.

The *Turnhalle* became a social, educational, and
cultural center of Kleindeutschland. By 1853, the
Halle housed a shooting gallery, fencing strips,
and twenty-three gymnastic teams. But the
members attended to more than sports: at the

annual Turnerfest, where *Turnvereine* from all over the country competed, prizes were also awarded for musical and theatrical presentations.

The Turners were so intensely concerned with educational matters that they founded their own schools. Carl Follen, a disciple of Turnvater Jahn, "father" of the Turners, had already opened the Roundhill School in Boston. There corporal punishment was abolished, students were divided by ability rather than by age, and competition was avoided if it encouraged some students at the expense of others. We don't know whether the *Turnverein* school in Kleindeutschland proceeded according to the same principles, but it was certainly a success: from two hundred students in 1853, it grew to more than twelve hundred students by 1884. Classes were taught entirely in German. But because no tuition was charged, it was eventually regarded as a public school, eligible to receive funds from the City.

The *Turnverein* and the German schools helped to preserve both the traditions and the language of the immigrants. Yet no matter how tenaciously many, perhaps most, of the Germans held on to their language and culture, their children suc-cumbed to what Theodore Roosevelt termed "ethnic turnover." The children would, he predicted, become "half, and the grandchildren in most cases wholly, Americanized."

Like the Germans, every immigrant group struggles with the tensions between integration and separation. Ultimately the struggling makes little difference. All finally give in to the zest of American English and the lure of American ways.

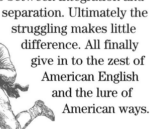

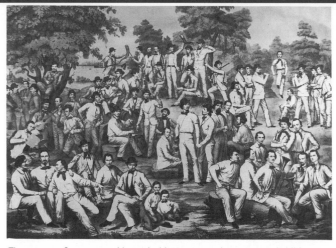

These young Germans—with musical instruments, dog, guns, and children—gathered at Jones's Wood on a long since leveled height above the East River. The nobility of their poses suggests that they were members of a lodge with one of the more high-minded mottoes.

10 Deutsch-Amerikanische Schützengesellschaft, 12 St. Mark's Place

At the German American Shooting Society members partied. "Shoot they did somewhere else." Although, as has been noted, many German immigrants were high-minded in the extreme, almost obsessed by issues of education, culture, and socialist reform, equally large numbers of them were far more dedicated to amusing themselves with sports and drinking and to re-creating a sense of the *Heimatland*, the homeland. Marksmanship in particular, a very German tradition, combined these interests. (Did women marksmen—and there were many of them—share their menfolks' alcoholic pleasures? Given the lack of segregation in saloons and at festivals, it seems likely.)

Other clubs were purely social; they brought together people from the same region, town, or neighborhood, giving them opportunities to speak their local dialect, to gossip, and to exchange news from home. The *Plattdeutsche Volksfest Verein*, an umbrella organization of close to a hundred clubs (some of them mutual-aid societies), was formed just for those purposes. Its primary activity was the yearly *Volksfest*— call it a week-long public merrymaking—at which as many as one hundred fifty thousand attendees happily celebrated their origins at Jones's Wood, a rustic area above the river in the east Sixties, or at other amusement parks outside the City.

As described in a German-language history of the *Volksfest Verein* published in 1892, the festival began as immigrants gathered "at the Beethoven Halle [210 East 5th Street] and at Tompkins Square, marched through Kleindeutschland along the main streets of downtown to the Christopher Street Ferry, through Hoboken to Union Hill. In a specially constructed farmhouse, a real wedding took place, as well as a christening."

From its street-level arches and sculpted heads to its imaginative roof line, the elaborate home of the *Schützengesellschaft* remains a memorial to the Germans of Kleindeutschland.

What this picture of Oswald Ottendorfer doesn't reveal is the breadth of the German community's interests. The front page of any issue of the *Staats-Zeitung* might carry news stories not merely from New York and Berlin but also from London, Paris, Johannesburg, and Havana.

Oswald. Ottendorfer.

11 12 Ottendorfer Library and Stuyvesant Polyclinic, 135 & 137 Second Avenue

Between St. Mark's Place and 9th Street on Second Avenue stand two lively reminders of the City's rich German heritage.

In #135, a building that once housed the *Freie Leseverein*, a free "reading club," is the Ottendorfer branch of the New York Public Library. It memorializes Oswald Ottendorfer, publisher of the *New-Yorker Staats-Zeitung*, leader of the City's many German-language newspapers.

The Polyclinic (originally the German *Poliklinik*), along with the *Leseverein*, was among Frau Ottendorfer's charitable concerns. Born Anna Behr, she first married August Uhl, then owner/publisher of the *Staats-Zeitung*. After Uhl's death in 1852 and for the next seven years, she managed the paper herself. In 1859, she married her dashing young editor, Herr Ottendorfer, and turned her attention to philanthropy. Aside from these two worthy institutions, she was particularly involved with the Isabella Home for aged women. (It operates today at the northern end of Audubon Avenue in Washington Heights.)

The Ottendorfer legacy of philanthropic concern lasted. Oswald's granddaughter, Carola

Woerishoffer, a labor inspector and reformer in the early 1900s, put up twenty-five thousand dollars (easily the equivalent of a third of a million dollars in today's money) as bail for the workers arrested in the shirtwaistmakers' strike of 1909 [see Jewish stop #2].

The *Poliklinik* opened in 1883 in the home of Dr. Samuel Kohn, an ear, nose, and throat specialist of Hungarian-Jewish ancestry, who began his practice in a City hospital on Blackwell's Island (today Roosevelt Island), a long spit of land in the East River which also contained a lunatic asylum, a jail, and a hospital for isolating victims of smallpox. The *Poliklinik* moved to its present location in 1884.

German doctors were, of course, highly esteemed. Educated in Germany, they were on the cutting edge of the profession, having experienced the finest medical training anywhere available in those years. Carl Beck, for example, who settled in the City in 1882 and was later to found and direct St. Mark's Hospital, was the first doctor in America to apply Dr. Roentgen's X-rays in diagnosis and cure. An even greater figure in Kleindeutschland, Abraham Jacobi—he brought the science of pediatrics to this country—became a president of the American Medical Association.

Only one of Frau Ottendorfer's charitable investments, this building, which housed both the *Leseverein* and the *Poliklinik,* was completed in 1883. *King's Handbook of New York* also credited it with a medical library of some three thousand volumes.

An artist working for *Frank Leslie's Illustrated Newspaper* drew this scene of the Tompkins Square riot for the January 31, 1874, issue. His sympathy with the strikers is clear. The protesters are shown not as a faceless mob but as distinct individuals, with visages depicting their ethnicity. Alone in the rear, astride his horse, an implacable policeman with billy club raised prepares to break someone's head.

13 | Tompkins Square Park

Tompkins Square Park, dubbed the *Weisse Garten* (White Garden), was pretty much the geographical center of later-day Kleindeutsch-land as well as the endpoint of the community's Sunday strolls. It was also the site of parades and, even then, of riots. In 1874, with the nation in the midst of a depression, some six thousand residents took to the streets to demand public works programs to relieve the worst unemployment and hunger. A bloody clash between the demonstrators (most of them immigrants) and the police ensued. A Kleindeutschland cigar maker, the fabled union leader Samuel Gompers [see stop #5], would described it years later in his autobiography:

> *[A] group of workers marched into the park from Avenue A. They carried a banner bearing the words "TENTH WARD UNION LABOR." Just after they entered the park the police sergeant led the attack on them. He was followed by police mounted*

*and on foot with drawn night-sticks.
Without a word of warning they swept
down the defenseless workers, striking
down the standard-bearer and using
their clubs right and left indiscrimi-
nately on the heads of all they could
reach.*

*Shortly afterwards the mounted police
charged the crowd on Eighth Street,
riding them down and attacking men,
women and children without discrimination. It was an orgy of brutality.*

Forty-six people were jailed, twenty-six of them
Germans, and Gompers himself is said to have
been so scarred by the violence that he became
forever opposed to radical unionism.

Leaders of the immigrant community—above all
German socialists, Freethinkers, Turners, cigar
makers, tailors, and cabinet makers—protested
the brutal police attacks. To no avail. Beyond
the general neighborhood of Kleindeutschland,
there was little sympathy for the workers.
Auguste Lilienthal's angry speech at a protest
meeting held at Cooper Union went unheard:

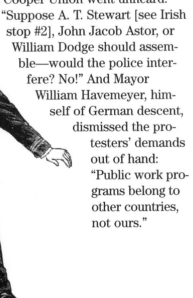

"Suppose A. T. Stewart [see Irish
stop #2], John Jacob Astor, or
William Dodge should assem-
ble—would the police inter-
fere? No!" And Mayor
William Havemeyer, him-
self of German descent,
dismissed the pro-
testers' demands
out of hand:
"Public work pro-
grams belong to
other countries,
not ours."

The Roman Catholic church of Most Holy Redeemer as it appeared in the 1870s.

14 | Most Holy Redeemer Roman Catholic Church, 173 East Third Street

Whether Catholic, Lutheran, or Reformed, the church in Germany played a very different role in nineteenth-century public life than did the churches in America. The German churches tended to be distanced from community concerns, and religious beliefs rarely connected with public issues, as they more often did in America, where, for example, preachers and practices might support the fight to abolish slavery. Thus, perhaps for more than 80 percent of German Christians, belief and observance tended to be perfunctory and superficial, and for many—especially the liberals and Freethinkers of the generation of '48—the church represented the enemy: tainted as collaborating with a repressive regime.

But certainly churches existed to serve that part of the German community not given over to secularism. The principal Catholic churches were the Most Holy Redeemer and its neighboring competitor, St. Nicholas Kirche (1833), the first German Catholic church in the City.

St. Nicholas thrived under the leadership of Johann Stephan Raffeiner, long the only German priest in New York. Before he left for Brooklyn in 1840, it served the largest congregation of any of the German churches—about a thousand members. After his departure, Most Holy Redeemer led in number of parishioners.

Among the other churches whose far fewer congregants were primarily or entirely German were Our Lady of Sorrows (103 Pitt Street), St. Matthew's (corner of Elizabeth and Broome streets), and two German Reformed churches (one at 129 Norfolk Street, the other on Avenue B at 5th Street), as well as Baptist (336 East 14th Street) and Presbyterian (296 Madison Avenue) churches and an Evangelical Mission (at Houston and Forsyth streets). The German Rationalist Church, founded in 1843, held services in Military Hall on the Bowery.

In a city where the Catholic hierarchy was and remains dominated by Irishmen, and where great numbers of possible congregants were more concerned with the here-and-now than with conditions in the next world, one might assume that the German churches had little function. But that would require overlooking the German passion for education. For parents uncomfortable with the nontraditional educational ideas of schools operated by the '48ers, there were spare-the-rod-and-spoil-the-child schools, some of which were quite successful.

At Most Holy Redeemer, for instance, the teachers were, according to Stanley Nadel, "men of solid, genuinely Catholic character. Old-fashioned instructors, they demanded obedience and order from the pupils, inside the schoolroom and outside." This was no more than one would expect: Father Müller of Most Holy Redeemer was fiercely conservative. When, in 1850, German tailors joined Irish tailors in a popular strike to protest a system that—for sixteen hour day, seven days a week—devalued their skills by requiring them to sew precut material (an early version of sweatshop labor), Father Müller denounced the strikers as antireligious.

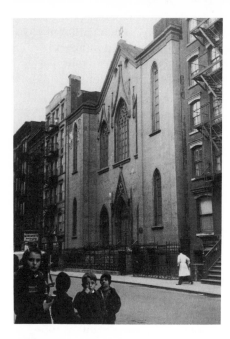

A snapshot of the substantial Norfolk Street synagogue erected in 1849-50 by the congregation of Anshe Chesed.

15 | Anshe Chesed, 172-176 Norfolk Street

To Congregation Anshe Chesed (People of Kindness) goes the honor of having erected the oldest still-standing Jewish house of worship in the City. The congregation formed in 1828; its building was completed in 1849. When its members moved out of the neighborhood, one by one other Jewish congregations moved in. In its time, the building also served congregations Ohab Zedek (Lovers of Justice) and Anshe Slonim (People of Slonim). The building survives today because artists have fought to establish their studios in it.

Such replacements were, and remain, unremarkable. Prior to1849, Jewish congregations on the Lower East Side, when they did not worship in storefronts or back rooms, always met in structures that had previously been consecrated as churches.

Anshe Chesed and Rodeph Shalom (Seekers of Peace), also German, also Orthodox, shared a rabbi for a time. He was Leo Merzbacher, who in

1845 joined with other advocates of modernization to create Temple Emanu-El, the first Reform congregation in the City. Theirs was a sharp break from traditional Judaism but one that was inevitable if a like-minded rabbi, having asserted his patriotism, could then say: "spiritually I am a German, for my inner life has been profoundly influenced by Schiller, Goethe, Kant, and the other intellectual giants of Germany."

The influence of the Freethinkers was also profound. In 1876, it led one German-Jewish rabbi, the liberal Felix Adler of Temple Emanu-El, to form the Ethical Culture Society. And again like the Freethinkers, its members were active in social and educational reform, eventually participating in the establishment of two settlement houses (University Settlement and the Hudson Guild) and a school which continues to flourish.

The spirit of modernization would affirm what was already true: that the Jewish sons and daughters of the eighteenth-century Enlightenment were little different from their Gentile neighbors in profoundly German Kleindeutschland.

For once, a newspaper minimized loss of life. At least 1,021 people—most of them women and children on a church outing—perished in the *General Slocum* disaster.

EPILOGUE

On Wednesday, June 15, 1904, an excursion steamer cruised up the East River from a dock on the Lower East Side. On it were over a thousand people from Kleindeutschland, mostly mothers and children of St. Mark's Lutheran Church on 6th Street east of Second Avenue. As the boat passed what is now Roosevelt Island, smoke was observed. Within minutes, caught in the tides of Hell Gate, the *General Slocum*—its cork life preservers and canvas fire hoses rotted—was ablaze. Most of its 1,331 passengers and crew died, burned to death or drowned in the worst disaster ever to be suffered in the City.

The heart went out of Kleindeutschland. The German community, broken by grief, moved away, primarily to Yorkville and to Astoria in Queens, leaving behind a monument to their dead children in Tompkins Square Park and their aging tenements to the immigrating Eastern European Jews.

10 STREET

4,6
M8, 101, 102, 103

E. 8TH · Ⓢ Ⓢ ASTOR PLACE · ST. MARK'S PLACE

WASHINGTON SQ. NORTH

WASHINGTON SQ PARK

⑯

E. 7TH

W. 4TH

W. 3RD

⑮

BROADWAY · LAFAYETTE · GREAT JONES · SECOND AVE · FIRST AVE

BLEECKER · MERCER

HOUSTON · Ⓢ

Ⓢ · BOWERY

PRINCE · ⑫ Ⓢ · ⑭

SPRING · ⑬ · ROOSEVELT PARK · ORCHARD

Ⓢ · KENMARE · DELANCEY

AVE OF AMERICAS (SIXTH AVE)

BROOME · DELANO · GRAND

⑪ · MULBERRY · SARA · HE

GRAND · GRAND

Ⓢ · CANAL · ELIZABETH

Ⓢ · MOTT

MANHATTAN BRIDGE

WEST BROADWAY · CHURCH · BROADWAY · CENTRE · BAYARD · BOWERY

WORTH · BAXTER · HUDSON

FOLEY SQ

⑩ (CHATHAM SQUARE)

⑨ ⑧ HENRY · MADISON

DUANE · ⑥ · ⑦ OLIVER · CATHERINE

READE · Ⓢ Ⓢ · Ⓢ · PARK ROW · JAMES ST

CHAMBERS · ② ③ · ST. JAMES PL · WA

④

MURRAY · Ⓢ · CITY HALL PARK · Ⓢ

⑤ · BROOKLYN BRIDGE

BARCLAY · ① · PARK ROW

4,5,6,N,R
M1,6,9,15,22,103,B51

FULTON

WORLD TRADE CENTER

LIBERTY · NASSAU · WILLIAM

Irish Heritage

On a frosty night over a friendly drink, a legend-spinning Irishman might tell of St. Brendan the Navigator, said to have preceded Columbus to the shores of North America by seven full centuries. Or he might tell of the Irishman who was a member of Columbus's crew. But neither adventurer would have reached Manhattan, whereas a small but significant number of Irish did live in Dutch and British New York before the American Revolution and more came after.

Our story begins later, however, primarily with the coming of the Irish to the City following the Napoleonic wars. The pressures of soaring population, depressed agricultural prices, extortionate jumps in tithes and taxes, and evictions by landlords set on turning tillage into grazing land—all these causes impelled the migration of laborers and landless farmers. And then came the infamous Famine years, when emigration turned into exodus.

Emigration didn't end when the Famine did. All told, during the century following 1815, almost five million Irish—and close to twenty-six million other Europeans—made their way to America.

A proud Irish youth emigrating from Queenstown harbor, his trunk neatly marked "steerage."

Prior to 1830, the Irish community of the City was religiously and socially diverse. It included merchants as well as indentured servants; Anglicans, Presbyterians, Methodists, and Quakers as well as Roman Catholics. They had some education, some capital, and some entrepreneurial skills. Like Henry and William James's Irish immigrant grandfather, who came to the City from County Cavan in 1789 and died a multimillionaire in Albany forty-three years later, some did very well indeed. James Duane, for example; the son of an immigrant, he became the City's first mayor in 1784.

Famine in itself was endemic in Ireland. According to the Poor Inquiry Commission established by the British government, the poorest fourth of the Irish population—out of a total of more than eight million people—regularly faced hunger every year, whether or not the potato crop failed. And the potato crop failed often—twenty-four times between 1728 and 1845.

But the potato blight that reached Ireland in 1845 was different in kind and extent. It had already ravaged crops in North America; it would strike England, Belgium, Holland, France, and Germany and would cause hardship everywhere. But in Ireland, where a third of the population depended for its diet solely on potatoes, and on a single variety at that—the "lumper," which was especially vulnerable to fungus—the blight was a disaster. There, among the already undernourished, hunger was accompanied by disease: typhus, "relapsing fever," bacillary dysentery, and cholera, as well as such noninfectious but hardly less dreadful conditions as hunger edema and scurvy.

Beginning in February 1847, Irish emigrants began to flood the docks on their way to Great Britain, Canada, Boston, and New York. Thousands, already carrying typhus or catching it in the hideously unsanitary conditions aboard ship, died on route.

Of those who reached these shores, the largest number disembarked in New York. The U.S. Commissioner for Emigration listed 52,946 Irish arriving in 1847 just between the months of May and December (as against 37,000 who landed in Boston). But before they could reach Manhattan, they had first to spend a thirty-day period in quarantine on Staten Island, for many had brought the fever with them. And of course the fever spread.

A mob attacking the Marine Hospital on Staten Island in 1858. Most of the quarantined were Irish who had been infected by yellow fever either before they left home or on the ships that brought them to New York.

The newcomers were not popular, not then, not later. In 1858, long after the Famine had abated, enraged and fearful residents of Staten Island burned down a hospital which held infectious immigrants.

It was not merely their contagion that aroused hostility. The Irish peasant newcomers—who kept on coming, coming—were, in addition, desperately poor, uneducated, unskilled, Roman Catholic, and sometimes not even English-speaking. (If they came from the west of Ireland, the only language many knew was Gaelic.)

Faced with signs reading "No Irish need apply"—more common in Boston than New York—the men took what they could get: ditch digging, stevedore work, manual labor. Indeed, they came almost to monopolize unskilled jobs, sometimes taking temporary leave of New York to build canals and railroads elsewhere in the country. The women—unique among immigrant groups, single Irish women immigrated in large numbers and, in the decades following the Famine, even outnumbered men—took in washing or worked as domestic servants and seamstresses.

And like immigrants before and after, they clustered together, matching only the Jews in their reluctance to give up the City, any city, for the great sweep of lands that composed America.

Their passion for urbanization seems odd; at home the emigrating Irish had been overwhelmingly rural. But accustomed to communal patterns of rural life, they would have been miserable on American farmlands that, even had they been affordable, were distant from one another and located in areas bereft of Catholic churches.

The Irish fleeing the Famine, as well as those who followed them, settled where the earlier Irish had already made base as early as 1830—on the Lower East Side.

Classified advertisements from an issue of the *New York Post* in 1830 reveal sharp historical truths: "Wanted, a Cook and a Chambermaid. They must be Americans, Scotch, Swiss, or Africans; none other need apply"; "Wanted—An American woman, white or black to work and wash…"; Wanted—A girl about 12 year old…; "Wanted a lad about 14 years of age…" Child labor, and no Irish wanted.

Irish Tour

1 ## St. Peter's Church, 22 Barclay Street

This building—the oldest Roman Catholic church in the City—dates from 1838. The congregation, however, was established in 1785 by an Irish priest just a year after repeal of the law barring priests from entering the state.

The initial two hundred members were ethnically mixed, although largely Irish. Dennis Mahan's immigrant parents had him baptized here in 1802, never imagining he would grow up to teach the art of war to Ulysses S. Grant at West Point. Elizabeth Seton, the first American-born saint, who converted after she was widowed, was baptized as a Roman Catholic in the parish. The Haitian-born Pierre Toussaint [see African stop #18] was married here, and a plaque on the building marks the centenary of his death.

Additionally notable is the plaque to Thomas Dongan, seventh governor of the colony of New York (1683–88). Dongan, an Irish Catholic sensitive to the discrimination faced by his coreligionists under English domination, granted the Charter of Liberties and Privileges. It established representative government in the colony, greatly expanded the colonists' religious freedom, and guaranteed them trial by jury.

2 ## A. T. Stewart and Co., 280 Broadway

This building (called the Marble Palace and later to contain the editorial offices and printing plant of the *New York Sun*) housed America's first department store. It was founded by Alexander Turney Stewart, who had emigrated from County Antrim in 1818 as a boy of fifteen. The store contained two acres of floor space and, at its height, employed three hundred salesmen and clerks.

At the height of its popularity, Stewart's "Marble Palace" played retailer to fifteen thousand customers a day buying $60,000 worth of merchandise. Such numbers were possible only because a throng of women were set to sewing the purchases.

2

cont.

Stewart's innovations were an open-door policy, counter stools on which customers could relax while they examined the merchandise under the eyes of the salesmen, and an arrangement—a "departmentalization"—that simplified both the stocking of myriad goods and the ease with which they could be located and viewed.

For more than twenty-five years, Stewart was the world's leading merchant. In New York City, he eventually required two stores to handle the hordes of people who wished to visit and buy. His second, "uptown" store, which opened for business in 1868, occupied an entire block at Astor Place. Twenty years after his death, the building became the site of Wanamaker's Department Store.

Although the average Irish immigrant could hardly afford to buy from him, Stewart remained sufficiently loyal to his countrymen to send a shipload of provisions back to Ireland during the Famine. He was not alone in his charity. It's estimated that gifts of money, food, and clothing from America totaled one million dollars, a sum that did not include what was sent to the victims privately.

3 | Emigrant Industrial Savings Bank, 49-51 Chambers Street

A savings bank expressly for Irish immigrants, the Emigrant Bank grew out of the Irish community's long tradition of assistance to newcomers.

The first such institutional structure of assistance, established in 1784, was the apolitical, nondenominational Friendly Sons of St. Patrick (its first president was a Presbyterian). Other societies followed, served (or failed to serve) their purpose, and disbanded. But the Irish Emigrant Society of New York, founded in 1841 by members of the Friendly Sons and backed by the Catholic clergy, lasted in the City until 1936.

Its purpose was to protest against and remedy the shipboard conditions their emigrating compatriots had to endure; to protect them against swindlers who found it easy to bamboozle and steal from the newly arrived greenhorns; and then to find them jobs (the employment office was at 29 Reade Street).

The bank—urged on the Society by the immensely influential Archbishop John Hughes, who had come to the City in 1838—provided, along with standard services, free remittance of money home to Ireland or to Britain, where great numbers of Irish continued to immigrate.

The remittances were most often used to pay the rent and the debts run up in the shops. The cost of steamship tickets to America—which varied in price over time: as high as twelve pounds from Liverpool to New York in 1816, down to thirty shillings from an Irish port to Quebec in the 1820s, and three pounds to New York in 1846—was covered by prepaid tickets. Friends or family members in America purchased the tickets from passenger brokers (who made a profit from the sale) and sent them on. Large sums were involved: during the second half of the century, a staggering one hundred million dollars is thought to have been paid out for such tickets.

The massive courthouse built by Boss Tweed became a symbol of the power and might of Tammany Hall and of the Irish ascendancy in City politics.

4 | "Tweed" Courthouse, 52 Chambers Street

This grand building—officially the Old New York County Courthouse—took twenty years to complete (1858–78). It is a monument to graft and was nicknamed for the chief grafter, William Marcy ("Boss") Tweed, whose ring made off with millions in construction costs.

Tweed was neither Irish nor Catholic, but during his time he controlled Tammany Hall, the Democratic, primarily Irish political club notorious for corruption. And although Tweed was thrown in jail in 1871–72 as a result of testimony from an Irish whistle blower, the rampant corruption did not halt.

One magnificent scam was revealed during Theodore Roosevelt's term as president of the Board of Police Commissioners. The then chief of police, one Thomas F. Byrnes, had made an international reputation for recovering stolen goods. If a person stood high enough on the social scale, no fur coat or diamond ring or piece of Georgian silver was ever in the hands of a burglar for long. The chief would promise to locate it, and a few days later—voilà!

4

cont.

Byrnes had no crystal ball. What he did have was an arrangement with the underworld. He permitted organized crime to go its own way, and in return, as a favor, the crime lords would unearth and return what had been lifted from the homes of the rich.

Reputation, however widely known, did not bring riches, and money, after all, was the name of the game. That Byrnes got from Wall Street. By steering criminal gangs away from the financial district, he was rewarded by Jay Gould and other high-level market manipulators with stocks and bonds that amounted to some three hundred fifty thousand dollars.

Edmund Morris, who described the corruption in his biography of Teddy Roosevelt, wrote, "Graft on so majestic a scale could not be expected of other police officers, but Byrnes's example was an inspiration to all."

5

Brooklyn Bridge

This extraordinarily beautiful steel-wire suspension bridge was designed by John A. Roebling, an engineer of genius who emigrated from Prussia in 1831. After his death in 1869, his son, Washington, oversaw the construction. When he became incapacitated three years later, his wife, Emily Warren Roebling, took over and managed the construction to its completion. But the actual building, of course, was done by thousands of laborers, most of them poor Irish immigrants— many of whom died from the bends (the same illness that felled Washington): nitrogen poisoning developed in the caissons required to set the deep foundations on the Manhattan and Brooklyn ends of the span.

When the bridge was to open in 1883, the Irish protested the date chosen. It was Victoria Day (May 24), birthday of the British monarch. Their threatened boycott didn't materialize. In fact, numerous Irish societies provided fireworks for the gala celebration.

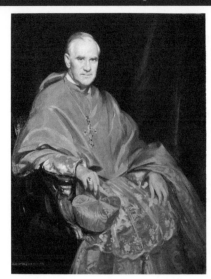

Much loved because of his concern for the laboring men and women of the City, Cardinal Hayes even defended the anarchist Catholic Worker movement initiated by the pacifist Dorothy Day.

6

St. Andrew's Roman Catholic Church, Centre Street and St. Andrew's Plaza

The original of this almost hidden church was established in 1842, here in what was once part of the Five Points area [see stop #10]. The building carries on its eastern exterior wall a bust of Patrick Hayes, who between 1919 and 1938 reigned as cardinal of the Archdiocese of New York.

Born in the then horrific slum area of Irish immigrant parents in 1867 and orphaned by the age of four, Patrick Hayes's life demonstrates another in the ways the impoverished Irish were able to advance in America. Like Al Smith [see stop 8], some rose through politics. Others—and Cardinal Hayes is the exemplar—succeeded through the church or the police department, both of which were Irish-dominated from top to bottom.

7 St. James Roman Catholic Church, 32 James Street

Completed in 1836, St. James was a major Irish church on the Lower East Side. At the close of the Civil War, it claimed as many as twenty-five thousand parishioners, a credible figure only when one understands that until the devotional revolution in the late 1850s, lay piety did not require regular church attendance.

The Church and Tammany Hall, the City's Democratic organization, would give the immigrants their most powerful affiliations in the new world. But fraternal organizations were hardly less important to the immigrants.

The Ancient Order of Hibernians combined fraternal association with religion and self-defense. Founded at St. James in 1836 during a time of mounting anti-Catholic activity, it was dedicated to protecting the Mass, the Priest, and the Church. But it also provided its members with opportunities to socialize and take courage in an alien environment.

Also affiliated with St. James and other parishes was the Father Mathew Total Abstinence Society (later the Roman Catholic Total Abstinence Society). But although Father Mathew's mission was popular—twenty thousand people were said to have taken the pledge from him in New York City alone—his was not the first or only society trying to exorcise "the curse of the Irish": the New York Catholic Temperance Association had already been founded in 1840 by Father Varela in the first parish of the Church of the Transfiguration [see stop #10].

Temperance societies continued to be strong enough numerically to affiliate with the St. Patrick's Day Parade. In 1863, for example, seven hundred abstainers, including a group from St. James, marched behind Father Mathew's banner. But one might guess that it was not temperance alone that attracted so many people. As one historian has pointed out, the societies were "respectable," in contrast to the highly suspect Irish nationalist secret societies. And in contrast to most Irish organizations in the City, temperance groups allowed women not merely to take an active part in their doings but also to hold office.

Two plaques on the church should be noted: one for the Ancient Order of Hibernians, the other commemorating Fr. Fèlix Varela, the immensely popular Cuban-born priest (and Cuban nationalist) who was known as "Vicar general to the Irish."

Son of the Lower East Side, Governor Al Smith (in derby) talking with a man who appears to be Herbert Lehman, a future—and four-term—governor of the state.

8 | Alfred E. Smith's Boyhood Home, 25 Oliver Street

Once an altar boy at St. James Church [see stop #7] and a pupil in its parochial school, Al Smith (1873–1944), four-time governor of New York State, lived here with his mother and sister after the death of his father in 1884.

The house (built c. 1830), in classic Greek Revival style, would have been built for a merchant and his family. By the time the Smiths moved in, however, it had become a multiple dwelling. Indeed, the overcrowding of single-

8

cont.

family houses on the Lower East Side led to the design and building of tenements, which on the same sized lot—twenty-five by one hundred feet—hold twenty-four families.

Born at 174 South Street—a house since demolished for another "advance" in urban dwelling places: the massive housing project—Smith inspired and energized generations of Americans through his efforts in support of the working class. With only six years of schooling—although he happily claimed the degree of F.F.M. (Fulton Fish Market)—Smith as governor enacted progressive labor, health, and housing legislation and achieved so impressive a record that he was nominated for the presidency of the United States in 1928. The electorate, fearful of Catholics and no doubt feeling superior to this man of the people who spoke with the street accent of a New Yorker, chose Herbert Hoover instead.

The riot of 1871 as sketched by a soldier of the 7th Regiment. Most of the carnage—forty-four civilians, two soldiers, and one policeman dead—was caused by the soldiers firing into the crowd of Irish immigrants who were protesting the parade of Orangemen flaunting their banner of (Protestant) King William.

9

Northern Hotel, Northeast Corner of Mott Street and Park Row

The Northern Hotel at this site was run by Jeremiah O'Donovan Rossa. Passionately anti-British, Rossa was the publisher of an extremist republican newspaper, *The United Irishman,* and a member in exile of the Fenian movement, a secret society dedicated to the establishment of an independent Ireland.

Like Rossa himslf, the hotel was said to seethe with hatred of the British, and it is likely that some among its residents joined the thousand or so men, largely soldiers returning from the Civil War, who hoped to foment an Anglo-American war by invading Canada. They knew they had no chance of success; they intended to make a statement. After eight Irishmen were killed and the statement had been made, they came home, as anti-British as ever.

Anti-British passions were further encouraged by a growing number of Irish-American newspapers, the most powerful of which was the *Irish World and Industrial Liberator,* first published from offices at 11 Frankfort Street. Founded in 1870 by Patrick Ford, an immigrant who had started out in Boston as a printer's devil for William Lloyd Garrison's abolitionist *Liberator,* this newspaper was, through the 1930s, the Irish equivalent of the *Jewish Daily Forward.* Like the *Forward,* it had a national readership and was an important voice of the American labor movement.

Irishmen also staffed, and not infrequently influenced, the nonethnic dailies published in the City. (It's been claimed that there was one Irish nationalist per paper.) Their support for Irish nationalism served to unify Irish Catholics, but it additionally alienated the City's small Protestant Irish community.

Rather than identifying with their Catholic countrymen, Irish Protestants either abandoned their ethnicity or organized into lodges as Orangemen

—affiliates of the Northern Irish society dedicated to promoting their own religious and political ascendancy.

There was no love lost between the two groups. In 1870 and 1871, elements of the two sides of the City's Irish community took their enmity into the streets on the occasion of parades commemorating the Battle of the Boyne, the 1690 victory of (Protestant) William of Orange over (Catholic) James II. In the 1871 melee, forty-seven people were killed and dozens more were injured.

Another section of Five Points, "Bandits' Roost" on Mulberry Bend, in a photograph by Jacob Riis. The original caption remarked that the derbied Irishman is "passing on his questionable inheritance" to Italian immigrants.

10 | Church of the Transfiguration, 25 Mott Street

As Protestant congregations abandoned the Lower East Side for neighborhoods less crowded with newly arrived immigrants, their now-empty houses of worship were bought by the incoming residents. The Catholic parish of the Transfiguration followed what remains common practice to this day.

Transfiguration, formed in 1836 by Father Varela, was originally housed in what had been a Presbyterian church on Chambers Street. In 1853, it bought this English Lutheran church building for thirty thousand dollars and within a few years so flourished that it was able to provide a tuition-free school for girls run by the Sisters of Charity and a similarly free school for boys run by the Christian Brothers. (In general, boys from Irish families were not given preference in education; girls attended school almost as often.) By 1862, the combined schools enrolled twelve hundred students, children of parents who worked as shoemakers and tailors, as butchers and grocers, as boardinghouse and liquor store owners, as blacksmiths, machinists, and foundry workers.

But many more parents were unemployed, or they worked as common laborers earning no more than three hundred dollars a year at a time when almost twice that amount was needed to maintain a working-class family. So even had there been seats enough for their children at Transfiguration, they could probably not have enrolled them. For the poor of all ethnic groups, school was a luxury, and the Sixth Ward, in which Transfiguration was located, was desperately poor. And unruly.

As early as the 1820s, the Sixth Ward's slum called Five Points was notorious for unrestrained behavior and squalor—and starvation. In his *American Notes* (1842), Charles Dickens, no stranger to the horrors of slum life, likened the area to the worst he'd seen in London.

79

10

cont.

Populated by prostitutes, thieves, murderers, drunkards, gamblers, and the abysmally poor, Five Points, named for the intersection where Columbus Park, Baxter Street, and Worth Street meet, was the home of the City's first street gangs. Two of the gangs were entirely Irish. According to Herbert Asbury, witty chronicler of City gangs, the Kerryonians, natives of County Kerry, "did little fighting; its members devoted themselves almost exclusively to hating the English."

More notorious were the Plug Uglies, whose appellation has come down to us as a lower-case, hyphenated noun meaning ruffian. (The name derives from their hats. Stuffed with wool and leather, and shaped like plugs, they served as protection during dust-ups.)

Irish gangs also took root on the Bowery. Herbert Asbury thought the Bowery toughs less ferocious than the gangs of Five Points, "although among them were many gifted brawlers."

It is easy enough to be amusing after the fact. Many of the men and boys who were the thugs of the Bowery and Five Points lived in total wretchedness—in an abandoned brewery or in unlit, unventilated, unheated, mud-floored cellars with the highest disease rates in the City. Were they supposed to respect or obey the laws of a city that permitted such conditions?

Perhaps it was just as well that they were illiterate, unable to read about how the rich lived. The diarist Philip Hone, for example, who did not like the Irish—"They are the most ignorant white men on earth," he wrote—recorded a shopping list for one of his dinner parties: "fourteen pounds of bass, two small turkeys, three pair of chickens, one pair of partridge, twenty-one pounds of hindquarter of veal, twelve pounds of mutton, and six pair of sweetbreads." Cost? No small sum for 1834—$17.31.

Arranged for the pianoforte under its original title, "Dixie" sold thousands of copies long before the tune was adopted as the Confederate anthem.

11 | Mechanics Hall, 472 Broadway

Owned by the Mechanics and Tradesmen Society of New York, the hall was for ten years home to the famous Christy Minstrels. After Christy retired in 1854, the stage was held by the Bryant Brothers Minstrels until the early 1860s.

The three brothers, sons of Irish immigrants, followed a minstrel tradition that had its formal beginnings in 1843 at the Bowery Amphitheater. Blackening their faces with burnt cork, telling jokes in Negro dialect, singing, and playing banjo, violin, and bone castanets in imitation of plantation slaves, the Bryants were among the pioneers of blackface minstrelsy, an immensely popular entertainment that survived into the twentieth century.

Offensive as the form appears today, blackface minstrelsy gave America some of its most memorable songs. Written for performance by the Christy Minstrels were Stephen Foster's "Old Folks at Home," "My Old Kentucky Home," and "Old Black Joe." The Bryants could boast of an equivalent contribution. In 1859 they were joined by an Ohio-born Irishman named Dan Emmett, a composer who had been violinist in the first blackface minstrel show. On the night

11

cont.

of April 4, Emmett introduced into the proceedings a new "walk-around." He called it "I Wish I Was in Dixie's Land." (Recent scholarship convincingly argues that Emmett lifted the song we have come to know simply as "Dixie" from two black musicians, Ben and Lew Snowden, who hailed from the same Ohio county.)

Almost as popular as the character types standard in the minstrel shows was the "stage Irishman," a loquacious, devil-may-care, drunken buffoon who arrived on the American stage at about the same time. (Even one of the Bryant brothers performed in the role.) Taken in stride by the workingman, the character was deeply resented by the Irish middle class, who were given to taking offense. Such a play as John Millington Synge's now classic *Playboy of the Western World*, for example, created riots both in Dublin (1907) and New York (1911).

Along with the names of his (or her) guests, a playgoer noted, "Riot—Wildly exciting." The next morning a newspaper reported "75 Cops Bounce a Rabble," adding in its headline that most of the bouncers were Irish, as were the captain and inspectors who commanded them.

The character type appreciated by all classes of the Irish was celebrated by Dion Boucicault, an Irish playwright much admired in New York. His 1875 play *The Shaughraun* (The Wanderer) offered an idealized figure—ourageous, daring, loyal, honest but wittily capable of stretching the truth, and moral to the core. In a charming irony, as young members of an amateur dramatic society at St. James Church, Jimmy Walker and Al Smith performed in this play. Walker, a later-to-be-disgraced mayor of New York, took the hero's role; Smith played the villain.

Years later, Hollywood, projecting an equally popular stereotype, made cinema history by casting New York's own James Cagney in the role of a cocky, streetwise antihero. The typical Irishman on today's stage is more often than not the dark, tortured protagonist in the dramas of Eugene O'Neill.

12 Hibernian and Montgomery Halls, 42 and 76 Prince Street

Hibernian Hall at #42 (the address has disappeared) and Montgomery Hall at #76 provided a variety of organizations with meeting rooms. Here, for example, both benevolent societies and military companies held their meetings.

The societies were formed so that even the poorest immigrants would not end up in potter's field without a Christian burial or headstone. Later, when the number of Irish in the City vastly increased, the societies grew in number but narrowed in inclusiveness. They organized along county and occupational lines. Stonecutters, masons, and journeymen tailors each had their own society, as did immigrants from Leitrim, Cavan, Fermanagh, and Sligo.

In a city where the mortality rate was sometimes higher than the birth rate—in the 1860s, with one death for every thirty-five in the population, the mortality rate was the highest in the western world—such organizations provided a small measure of security. They not only buried the dead but also paid out sick benefits and a form of life insurance to survivors. For monthly dues of twelve and a half cents in 1850, a member of the Laborers Union would receive two dollars a week in sick benefits and his family a lump sum of fifteen dollars for funeral expenses should he die. Other societies set higher monthly dues but provided higher benefits: three dollars a week for the sick, twenty-five dollars for the funeral.

12

cont.

The benevolent societies were also instrumental in putting the St. Patrick's Day Parade on a more organized basis. When eleven new marching groups joined the 1851 parade, six societies formed a central organization called the Convention of Irish Societies. The convention's headquarters alternated between the halls at #42 and #76 for over twenty years while its members worked out the increasingly complicated details of each year's parade.

Also headquartered at the two halls were the volunteer militia companies popular among young Irishmen who, as "aliens," were rejected by the native militia prior to the Civil War. The reason for their popularity is blurred by time. Perhaps a volunteer company gave the man who trained and drilled in it hope that he could protect his community against growing nativist attack. Perhaps it allowed him to dream that one day he could participate in freeing Ireland from the hated British. Perhaps it provided him with no more than an opportunity to dress up in fancy uniform and have a sociable night out. All the reasons are plausible.

By the time of the Civil War, the "alien" militia-men had become acceptable–the 69th Regiment of the New York State Militia, entirely composed of local Irish companies, received its baptism under fire at the first battle of Bull Run. Although the Union side lost, the "Fighting 69th" returned to an uproarious welcome and were cheered, street after street, as they marched from the Battery up Broadway to Union Square, then down the Bowery to the old Essex Market, where a new armory had been completed.

The Irish regiments compiled an imposing record during the Civil War, but they were not fighting and dying to end slavery. They were bitterly opposed to abolition, which they associated with radicalism, American nativism, and Great Britain. No, the Irish were not about to look sympathetically on Mr. Lincoln or Mr. Lincoln's war.

But when the South seceded and fired on Fort Sumter, the Irish took up the cause of Unionism. According to Maldwyn Jones, "Irrespective of its views on slavery each ethnic group simply gave its loyalty to the section [of the country] of which it was a part."

So the Irish fought magnificently on the battle-fields of the war. But in New York City, they were the leading players in the appalling Draft Riots of 1863, when for four days mobs burned, looted, cut telegraph wires, destroyed railroads, set fire to the Colored Orphan Asylum (at 43rd Street and Fifth Avenue), and lynched blacks from lampposts.

Why? To begin with, the Irish of the City feared that freed slaves would compete with them for the same backbreaking jobs they themselves toiled at. Add to that the ever-present racism that infected the country and their experience of seeing blacks used as strikebreakers on the rail-roads and the docks. Finally, the Irish felt they

Tuesday, April 23, 1861: the Irishmen of the Fighting 69th, still a state militia, depart for their initial engagement—the first battle of Bull Run. Old St. Patrick's Cathedral, with its graveyard, is at the right.

were particularly disadvantaged by this first federal draft in the nation's history. It could be escaped by paying into the U.S. treasury the sum of three hundred dollars. But what poor man—and in New York "poor" and "Irish" were synonymous—had so great a sum?

Surely the Irish felt that the draft was directed at the only Irish civilians remaining: married men with dependents.

It should also be noted that rioting is a poor man's standard form of expression, and it was used both by and against the Irish. Between 1806 and 1871, eleven recorded riots in the City involved either attacks on Catholic churches or fighting between Catholics and Protestants [see stop #9].

Before it was walled around, the original St. Patrick's Cathedral dominated a genteel Mulberry Street.

Old St. Patrick's Cathedral, 260-264 Mulberry Street

Old St. Patrick's–so called to distinguish it from the 1878 cathedral on Fifth Avenue–was the first Catholic cathedral in New York State and the second Catholic church in the City. It was founded in 1809, dedicated in 1815, burnt in 1866, and rebuilt in 1868.

During that period, Catholicism in the City was experiencing astonishing growth. When this Mulberry Street cathedral was dedicated, the number of New York Catholics stood at fifteen thousand. By 1865, half of all the people in the City were Catholic (some two-thirds of them Irish, the remainder largely German), and it would not be partisan to say that only a few years later New York became a Catholic city: Tammany Hall and City Hall were both run by Irish Catholics. If the big money was in the hands of socially prominent Protestants, the day-to-day power was in the hands of unfashionable Catholics.

From the beginning, however, Irish Catholics were objects of suspicion, bigotry, and active aggression. (Old St. Patrick's was twice threatened by mobs.) Over and above the fear of being overrun by "foreigners" who owed allegiance to the pope (language familiar in political debates right through John Kennedy's campaign for the presidency), there was in New York City the divisive issue of education.

In the earliest years, schools were the responsibility of religious institutions. By 1805, recognizing that many poor children had no connection with any religion, the state made provision for "common schools," and they, along with schools run by denominations, were now to receive public funding.

Without going into the immensely complicated history, by the 1830s the schools receiving money from the state had come under the jurisdiction of the Public School Society, whose

The same building served as headquarters for both the Public School Society and its successor, the Board of Education. The idyllic scene belies the conflicts always surrounding public education in the City, whether on Grand Street in the nineteenth century or on Livingston Street, Brooklyn, today.

13

cont.

members were Protestant and whose views of education were imbued with Protestant attitudes. The Catholics–Irish and German both–objected to daily readings from the King James version of the Bible and to the often derogatory slant on their religion taught in these schools. They also wanted their children to be educated in their own faith, with teachers and a curriculum imbued with Catholic values. Hence the development of a separate parochial school system.

The support of the parochial system was a major social and financial undertaking for a poor community–by 1858 it was valued at more than two million dollars. But despite its size, it encompassed no more than a third of all the school-age Irish children. Even so, few Irish youngsters lacked for a Catholic education. They could attend public ward schools. Theoretically nondenominational, the ward schools were supervised by locally elected boards and staffed by local teachers. In the most heavily Irish wards on the Lower East Side, that meant a Catholic board, Catholic teachers, and, for all practical purposes, a Catholic education.

The results of the understandable importance attached to Catholic education, tied up as it intricately was with the survival of ethnicity, were not totally beneficial, however. Catholic schools, whether parochial or public, slowed Irish integration into the wider community. Nor did they allay native-born and even immigrant Protestant suspicions of the "subversiveness" of Catholicism, a reputation fed by Archbishop Hughes, who in 1850 had grandly announced in *Freeman's Journal* that his mission was to "convert the world, including the inhabitants of the United States, the people of the city and the country, the officers of the Navy, the Marines and the Army, the Senate, the Cabinet, the President and all."

Those who did not recognize blarney when they heard it banded together in such short-lived nativist organizations as the Know-Nothings and, later, the American Protective Association, organizations that in opposing immigration, most especially by Catholics, renewed an ugly strain of xenophobia that dated from the 1790s and rejected what would be the nation's greatest strength, its genius for inclusivity.

14 Hibernian Hook and Ladder Fire Company, No. 18, 195 Elizabeth Street

Prior to 1865, when the City professionalized its fire service, volunteer companies handled all fires. This now-apartment house was built in 1862 as quarters for one of the many Irish companies.

The firemen had their work cut out for them: horses to feed and curry, streets thick with pushcarts to traverse, people to rescue from tenements that were not yet required to have fire escapes, fires to subdue despite winter cold that would freeze the water in their hoses. The job, never easy, was harshly difficult in those days.

14

cont.

But the folklore of the City memorializes the fun and games. The volunteer fire stations, which developed along ethnic and religious lines, combined social club, sports club, and political hangout. And all too frequently the sports were no more than races between companies to arrive first at a fire. "They were fiercely competitive," wrote Herbert Asbury, "now and then duking it out for the privilege of extinguishing the blaze and letting the unlucky building char and crumble as the fight raged on...."

Skills of leadership were also bred in the firehouses, as were small but loyal constituencies willing to stuff ballot boxes for a fellow firefighter. William Tweed and "Honest John" Kelly, who took over Tammany Hall when Tweed was imprisoned, began their political careers as members of volunteer fire companies.

WAITING FOR THE PAPERS.

Poorly nourished and ill-clad, newsboys rose before dawn and waited for the morning papers to roll off the presses.

Mission of the Immaculate Virgin for the Protection of Homeless and Destitute Children, 380 Lafayette Street

Completed in 1881, the ten-story building at this site was built to house four hundred homeless and destitute children. In addition to living quarters, the structure contained a chapel, classrooms for the teaching of both job skills and basic education, a library, and the first rooftop playground in the City. Cooking was done in the basement on a double-range stove. The hundred-gallon tank for making soup also supplied the neighborhood poor.

Spurred into existence by the advent of Protestant agencies run by proselytizing reformers, Catholic charity was practical. Following the traditions of European Catholicism, its purpose was to alleviate suffering, not to improve conditions. And there was suffering enough to keep it busy.

One of the common sights in nineteenth-century New York was the presence of children on the streets–earning pennies by peddling, selling newspapers, blacking shoes, sweeping crosswalks, holding horses, running errands, foraging for rags and scrap they could sell to the junkman. Middle-class reformers–who rarely understood working-class culture and who believed fervently in what has come to be termed "family values," with a father at work and a mother at home tending the little ones–were appalled. To them it seemed as if the parents were deliberately uncaring; if not simply ignorant, then obviously immoral.

But since paying one's rent on time could literally mean the difference between life and death, every able-bodied person in a household had an obligation to contribute to the rent, which was rarely cheap although what it bought was standardly dreadful. For a space sometimes no larger than ten feet by twelve, with a ceiling so low that adults often could not stand upright, rents

Not Father Drumgoole's home for newsboys but indicative of what it must have resembled. Their schooling would have taken place at night, after the evening papers had been sold.

ran from five to seven dollars a month. We're told that profits to the landlord could range from 17 percent to over 100 percent.

With limited job opportunities, periodic depressions, and seasonal unemployment, the man of the house often could not earn enough to make the rent payments. Women had no choice but to work. And given the frequency of the death of adult wage earners–cholera, typhus, tuberculosis, and industrial accidents were all commonplace–children not only worked on the streets but might also live there, orphaned or abandoned by parents unable to cope with the strain of urban life and wallowing in mental illness, alcoholism, or drug addiction.

The best-known job for youngsters was selling newspapers. In 1871, a hundred papers brought in fifty cents. Working as long as fourteen hours a day for a six-day week, a newsboy might earn all of three dollars. (If he were well positioned and selling to the affluent, he'd also receive tips.) Had there been a place for him other than alleys and doorways, he could afford to pay for lodgings.

Fr. John C. Drumgoole, an Irish immigrant, began housing newsboys in 1871 in a spot on Warren Street. Within a decade, the need for larger facilities was more pressing than ever, and Father Drumgoole established his Mission of the Immaculate Virgin on this corner. It was supported by the members of the worldwide St. Joseph's Union, who contributed twenty-five cents a year in dues, and by the profits from a magazine called *The Homeless Child*, both set up by Drumgoole.

Six months after the building opened, Father Drumgoole began construction of a second mission. (It is still in operation as Mount Loretto on Staten Island.) The youngest children were sent there, leaving the Manhattan building for working boys. By 1886, Father Drumgoole was caring for twelve hundred children at a time.

By necessity, women were also the object of Catholic charity. The Institution of Mercy, opened in 1849 in St. Catherine's Convent on the corner of Houston and Mulberry streets, was the first to direct itself to homeless and/or unemployed women–*virtuous* women who, the good Sisters feared, might lose their virtue without the Convent's ministrations. In its first year it found jobs, mostly in domestic service, for over twelve hundred women, and it regularly gave refuge to an average of one hundred women a night.

In 1857, another order of Irish and Irish-American nuns established a convent on 14th Street. Its mission was with "unchaste" women, that is, with those who had become prostitutes.

Recent scholarship sheds important light on the issue of prostitution among immigrant women in the City. Studying an 1855 report on the causes of prostitution, Christine Stansell observes that "destitution" was not the only reason given by the "fallen women" interviewed. Almost a quarter cited "inclination." She goes further: without for a moment minimizing the effect of poverty on occupational behavior, Stansell notes that:

> *a variety of factors led women into the trade. The daughter of a prosperous ship carpenter could end up on the streets because she was orphaned and left to support herself; she could also use prostitution as a way to escape a harsh father's rule...A married woman might even hazard the prospects of a hand-to-mouth*

independence, supported in part by prostitution, rather than submit to a drunken and abusive spouse.

"Prostitution was neither a tragic fate, as moralists viewed it (and continue to view it), nor an act of defiance, but a way of getting by, of making the best of bad luck," Stansell affirms. Prostitution and casual sex not only paid well—considerably better than almost any other female occupation—it also allowed for a degree of freedom. Not all poor women chose to be victims.

Saloons were often voting places, and one can be sure that Clancy and Kelly garnered every vote cast by the patrons of this one. Both Irishmen were "Regular Democrats," and "Honest John" was Tweed's successor as the leader of Tammany Hall. No other credentials were needed.

16

McSorley's Old Ale House, 15 East 7th Street

According to the sign in the window, this bar was opened in 1854 by John McSorley. According to Richard McDermott, a "saloon scholar" who publishes the delightfully informative *New York Chronicle*, McSorley didn't arrive in the City until 1855, and his bar wasn't recorded in a City directory until 1862.

City dwellers often benefited from having their pockets picked by Tammany Hall: Boss Tweed's courthouse still stands, and help was instantly extended in emergencies, in this case to families bereaved by the sinking of the *General Slocum*.

Whatever the case, this ale house was established by McSorley, an immigrant from County Tyrone, who would serve in the Civil War as a member of the 69th Regiment, and it may be the City's oldest extant Irish bar. (If it isn't, McDermott says the Bridge Cafe, nestled beside the Brooklyn Bridge at 279 Water Street, appeared in the records in 1794—without, of course, any indication of its owner's ethnicity.)

McSorley's, however, is a City institution. A longtime favorite watering hole for writers, reporters, and Tammany pols, it made the headlines most recently in 1970 when, finally and not without protest—the original McSorley's maxim was "Gentlemen cannot drink in tranquility with ladies present"—it opened its doors to women.

What is significant about McSorley's and the other Irish saloons it represents is that they used to double as information centers and hiring halls. Men in search of work could learn of jobs at the pub, and since most of the prolific public works projects in nineteenth-century New York were subject to patronage, the local ward boss was the person to see about getting hired. More often than not, the ward boss and the saloonkeeper were the same man. Buying a drink at his bar was merely reciprocal business.

16

cont.

In turn, the publican would treat his customers to drinks in expectation that, come election day, they would stuff the ballot boxes for his candidate. It was a cozy connection—and profitable. Theodore Roosevelt would later write of the scene, "the ward politician, the liquor seller, and the criminal alternately preyed on one another and helped one another to prey on the general public."

Although reformers fulminated, the ward politicians achieved remarkable success. In the days before institutionalized welfare, they provided not just the proverbial Christmas turkey and the scuttle of coal but also help in meeting the rent or bail. They, or the smaller fry called "ward-heelers," would turn up at fires to dispense aid; if the victims were not already Democrats, they'd soon join them.

This practical benevolence combined with well-honed organizational skills dating back to the 1820s, when Daniel O'Connell familiarized the rural population of Ireland with political activity, gave Irish-American political bosses an edge. They held and kept power in Manhattan and the outer boroughs until Fiorello La Guardia was elected mayor in 1933 on the Republican–City Fusion line.

EPILOGUE

With the continuing shifts of ethnic power in the City, only one politician of Irish birth—William O'Dwyer—would become mayor for the remainder of the century. But in recent years, as the Irish have settled in the suburbs, they have faced a larger electorate and won senatorial seats, not to mention a governorship. And in the City itself, Irishmen still claim the cardinal's throne in St. Patrick's Cathedral, Irish cops still rise to head the police department, firehouses still cook up corned beef and cabbage, and all the City claims Irish inheritance on St. Patrick's Day.

Built of granite in 1838, St. Peter's Church appears here after the encroaching neighborhood hemmed it in.

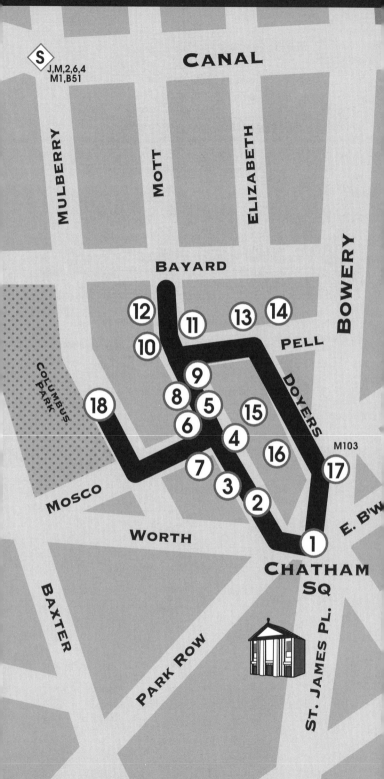

Six Tours of the **Lower East Side**

CANAL

S
J,M,2,6,4
M1,B51

MULBERRY

MOTT

ELIZABETH

BOWERY

BAYARD

12 11 13 14

10

PELL

9

18 8 5

6 15

DOYERS

4

7 16

M103

3 17

2

MOSCO

1

WORTH

E. B'W'Y

BAXTER

CHATHAM SQ

PARK ROW

ST. JAMES PL.

COLUMBUS PARK

Chinese Heritage

Of the six major ethnic groups to have come to the Lower East Side before World War I, only two were ever set apart by the law: the Africans, who could be enslaved in New York until 1827, and the Chinese. Of all immigrant groups wishing to work in America in the nineteenth century, only the Chinese specifically came to be excluded from entering the country.

They left China for good reasons. Their country had been and was suffering from internal rebellions, bad harvests, and floods. As a result, untold numbers of Chinese were killed, made homeless, starved. Additionally, a growing population had created sharp competition for arable land. And many of those who had land lost it because of cruelly high taxes.

Seeking a better life, some Chinese first sought it in other areas of China; the Chinese government initially opposed their going elsewhere. After that opposition died, those from the Canton area went as far afield as Hawaii, where they might earn as little as (as much as?) five dollars a month on the sugar cane plantations, Mexico, South America, the Caribbean, and—once they learned about the Gold Rush and the shortage of labor—California.

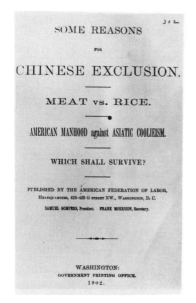

A repugnant indication of how organized labor viewed the Chinese, the title page of this defense of the exclusion acts carries the name of Samuel Gompers, president of the American Federation of Labor, and himself an immigrant.

L ike the Italians, the Chinese generally didn't plan to remain in the United States. Their idea was to come as "sojourners," to work hard, to send money home, and, after a few years, to return to farms and villages lying within a hundred miles of the city of Canton in the southeastern province of Guangdong, where their wives and families still lived.

Unlike the Italians, however, who were recruited for work in the United States by *padroni* [see the Italian introduction], the Chinese came on their own. They either paid their own way or, more frequently, borrowed the money for transportation from a broker through what was known as the "credit-ticket" system. Once employed in the States, they repaid the loan with interest. Although it is still often thought that the Chinese who arrived on the West Coast docks had been kidnapped for the express purpose of coercing them into labor in the mines and on the railroads, that appears not to be the case. In China, a laborer could earn five dollars a month at most; in California, he could earn six times that amount. These sojourners were men who made choices.

We're told that those who went to California arrived rather too late to strike it rich in the gold fields, although some continued at mining in Nevada and Wyoming throughout the century. Most, however, turned their energies to other work, first in San Francisco and then up and down the coast from Los Angeles to Seattle.

When the jobs were completed, out of poverty, loneliness, and the need to protect themselves from the overt hostility of the surrounding communities, they crowded into their own enclaves–just as the Germans, the Irish, the Jews, and the Italians had or would. The Chinese referred to their "Chinatowns," their self-sufficient villages within cities, as "the streets of the Tung people," so called because the great city of Canton first became part of China during the Tung Dynasty (619-907 A.D.).

By the 1860s, a second wave of Chinese were building the last leg of the transcontinental railroad, from San Francisco to Promontory Point, Utah. The twelve thousand Chinese workers—at thirty-one dollars per month—made up 90 percent of the workforce. When that terrible toil was completed in 1869, they sought new locations and other jobs—building levees and reclaiming marshlands, working in salmon canneries and textile mills and in factories producing silk and gunpowder. Little by little, smaller and larger pockets of Chinese could be found from California and the other western states all the way to New Jersey, Massachusetts, and New York. Some were coaxed to the post-Civil War South, where plantation owners intended another "inferior" minority to replace the slaves.

The geographic dispersal speaks to the determination, hardiness, and sheer guts of the Chinese. It also casts light on the ugliness they encountered, especially in the West, where they faced fierce prejudice and—as happened in California (1871), Colorado (1880), Wyoming (1885), and Oregon, Washington, and Alaska (1886)—open violence. One example, conveniently forgotten for more than a hundred years, occurred in the northeast corner of Oregon in 1887. There thirty-one Chinese gold miners were slain, some fifty thousand dollars of their gold was stolen, and not one of the six butcher-thieves paid the penalty. More to the point after all these years, the massacre, described as the worst ever of Chinese by white men in this country, has still been unredeemed by so much as a plaque or a line in the textbooks.

To the Anglo-Saxon, the Chinese skin color was unfamiliar, their eyes seemed to slant, their spoken language was a puzzle, their script unreadable. Even to the first- and second-generation European immigrants who had so recently preceded them to America—at least to those who had no opportunity to exploit their willingness to work hard—the Chinese became objects of fear and hatred.

Labeled "coolies" from their word for "hard labor," the Chinese were viewed as competitors, as mysterious, queue-wearing "Mongols" who consented to toil for wages far below those demanded by "real" Americans. There was some truth to the accusation. Given that broad occupational opportunities were closed to the Chinese because of racial prejudice and that lack money kept them from turning jobs down, they *did* work for less, but not necessarily by choice. Berkeley professor Ronald Takaki tells of a strike of five thousand Chinese against the Central Pacific Railroad in the 1860s, a strike not broken until their food supplies were cut off. It's also worth noting that the American labor movement, focused on its own goals, was not concerned to include Chinese workers. On a number of occasions, in fact, organized labor was intent on excluding them.

Eventually the Chinese not only dispersed but also made further occupational adjustments. Essentially they opted out of the regular labor force. Some continued as small-scale entrepreneurs. Most took up low-capital, labor-intensive "Chinese" occupations like cooking, gardening, domestic and laundry services, and waiting on tables.

Their flexibility didn't matter. In 1880, the flow of Chinese laborers was regulated. By an act of Congress in 1882 under pressure from the State of California, admission of Chinese workers was suspended. Only teachers, students, merchants, and short-term visitors were now permitted entrance. And certainly they could not be citizens. That restriction had been passed by Congress in 1790; the law stipulated that only white people could become naturalized citizens of the infant republic.

In 1884 still more restrictions were imposed. In 1888, President Cleveland signed legislation making it virtually impossible for any Chinese to return to the States if he left even briefly for home, although loopholes continued to exist for merchants and their families. Women, aside from those related to merchants, were forbidden entry.

The earliest date for Chinese in New York City is 1784; they were sailors and merchants. Those who didn't return to China married non-Chinese, changed their names, and became part of the City's ethnically unidentifiable. The City's first documented Chinese—he called himself William Brown and was married to an Irish woman—arrived in 1825.

By 1859, Chinese merchants and sailors numbered one hundred fifty. By 1870, their numbers rose to somewhat more than two thousand. Between 1880 and 1890, the population of New York's Chinese contingent tripled and then continued to grow, in part through a clever tactic called "paper families." A man in the country legally would sell his documents so that his "son" could be admitted. And to prove that the person seeking entry was a merchant, forged documents would show that he was a shareholder in a (fictitious) Chinatown business. But the community remained lopsided. Because it was men—manual laborers—who had been wanted in America at the beginning, women didn't come. Then, with the exclusion acts, women couldn't come. As a result, in 1890, only about 3.5 percent of the approximately one hundred ten thousand Chinese in the country were female. And although the percentage would increase over time, even as late as 1940 the ratio of men to women was not yet four to one.

In December 1943, presumably as a gesture of friendship to an ally during World War II, the Chinese exclusion acts were finally repealed. But there was a catch: in place of exclusion, a quota—one-sixth of 1 percent of the Chinese counted in the 1920 census. Given the various acts of exclusion, this meant that a maximum of one hundred and five Chinese people could enter as legal immigrants each year.

In 1965, Congress liberalized the immigration and nationality laws. The results are beyond the purview of a heritage guide, but no one who walks the streets of the Lower East Side today can be unaware that another, larger body of Chinese have come to live beside the Hispanics who replaced the previous inhabitants, Eastern European Jews and Italians. It is a good sign. The Lower East Side lives.

Since 1909 the cacophonous crossroads for traffic wending back and forth between Manhattan and Brooklyn, Chatham Square was probably never as serene as depicted in this 1866 rendering. Long before the Manhattan Bridge was built, sailors, immigrants, and merchants from many lands would have jostled and elbowed as they debouched into the Square from the docks nearby.

Chinese Tour

1 | Chatham Square

Until 1803, when a park was built here, Chatham Square—today a traffic nightmare described by the Municipal Art Society as "an urban design disaster"—was the site of a deep pond fed by spring water. By 1816, the park was abandoned in favor of the Boston Post Road, and hotels and rooming houses sprang up around the perimeter. When the Chinese from the mines and railroads of the West began coming to the City in 1875, one of the first locations they chose was the lower end of Mott Street at Chatham Square, then an Irish neighborhood. Housing was cheap, and the constant flow of travelers by road and sea required the services the Chinese set up to supply: food and laundry.

Mott Street

New York's nineteenth-century Chinatown developed along Doyers and Pell streets and along the stretch of Mott Street between Pell and Chatham Square. Mott Street was the main, if narrow, thoroughfare; it was here that the earliest Chinese restaurants, groceries, and joss houses were established.

The most gorgeously decorated and illuminated buildings in Chinatown during the 1890s were the restaurants, which catered not only to the local population but also to thrill-seeking New Yorkers and their guests from out of town. In every case, the food served was Cantonese, and all the restaurants—there were dozens of them—soon had chop suey available for unknowing tourists. (Literally "miscellaneous pieces," chop suey is a hodgepodge of a dish that self-respecting Chinese would never think to prepare for themselves. It should gratify local pride to learn that the dishonor of invention goes to Li Hung Chang, who first concocted it in 1896, in Chicago.)

By catering to tourists, Chinatown fit neatly into the economy of the Lower East Side. Within walking distance, tourists could take

To assure themselves of American patrons, most of the restaurants on the street included either the words "chop suey" or "chow mein" in their names. Not to be outdone, one (third from the left) strove for originality by calling itself "Lichee Wan." The tower marks the Church of the Transfiguration.

their entertainments at black-faced minstrel shows performed by Irishmen, drink German lager beer, and visit Jewish-run gambling houses. With the coming of the Chinese, tourists could add joss houses and restaurants serving unfamiliar food—a still richer taste of the exotic.

3 Port Arthur Restaurant, 7 Mott Street

The Port Arthur, one of the largest and most elaborately decorated of the old restaurants, stood at 7 Mott Street, now the location of the Kam Kou Supermarket. Established about 1896 in what was formerly a mattress and bedding factory, it sat two hundred diners at a time at carved teakwood tables and boasted rosewood archways, tapestries hand-woven of silk, and marble flooring—all imported from China.

Above the restaurant, on the third floor of #7, was the headquarters of a relatively short-lived secret organization called the Kaoshen (High Mountain) Club. One of a number of political clubs organized in America and dedicated to reforming the Chinese government, it published a newspaper—the *Chinese Reform News*—ran a bank and, like other branches of the movement, a military school.

Today used as a storage space for the supermarket at street level, the third floor was, for a brief time in 1896, a stopover for Sun Yat-sen, the Cantonese doctor who would become the founder and provisional president of the Chinese Republic in 1912. The exclusion acts being what they were, in all likelihood Dr. Sun was traveling on a false passport, passing himself off, as he would do on other such occasions, as having been born in Hawaii.

From these rooms, Dr. Sun personally organized a New York branch of his then secret revolutionary party (later to evolve into the Guomindang) and recruited members of the community to return to China and join him in a

Within the Port Arthur Restaurant, the chef and his assistants pose for their pictures. Sent home to Canton, this publicity shot would also demonstrate how healthy the men looked and how well they were succeeding in America.

democratic revolution to overthrow the Qing dynasty. It is not known how many New York Chinese took up the offer. What we do know is that throughout the years they, along with vast numbers of overseas Chinese, showed extraordinary concern for the welfare of their homeland and substantially contributed to appeals aimed at strengthening and uniting the country.

The oldest Chinese paper in New York, the *Chinese Reform News,* was first published on March 10, 1904. Like most ethnic newspapers, it focused on news of direct concern to its readers: what was happening in other enclaves in America and, of still greater importance, what was going on in their homeland.

Chinese Consolidated Benevolent Association, 16 Mott Street

The most important location in Old Chinatown, the second floor of #16, housed the Chinese Consolidated Benevolent Association (CCBA), formed in 1883 to oversee rival groups of Chinese who had grouped together in a variety of organizations held together by shared sur-name [see stop #10], or originating village or district, or fraternal principles. This supervisory association, under the alternating presidency of the heads of the two largest district associations [see stop #11], had the power to tax, to regulate commerce, and to arbitrate the endless conflicts among the groups.

The services it performed were especially nec-essary because the Chinese had good reason to distrust American courts, which were not always places where "foreigners" could expect equal justice. On the West Coast, for example, Chinese (as well as blacks, mulattos, and Indians) were legally barred from testifying against white men. And in addition to the lan-guage barrier, white judges and juries would have had no notion of the principles or com-plexities underlying the conflicts.

The CCBA, now headquartered at 62 Mott Street, still retains a modicum of power in the community, functioning as the unofficial City Hall of Chinatown. But it has grown increasingly weak for reasons having to do

Dr. Sun Yat-sen visited Chinatown in 1896 to recruit support for the nascent Guomindang, the political party based on his Three Principles: anti-imperialist nationalism, democracy, and socialism.

with changes in Chinatown's demography. College-educated social activists have returned to the community. Skilled at petitioning for federal and state aid, they are not dependent on the traditional associations for funding.

Additionally, the CCBA is unable to represent the interests of the thousands of ethnic Chinese who have emigrated from previously unrepresented geographical areas overseas.

In the 1920s, the CCBA ceded some space on the second floor of #16 to the Chinese Hand Laundry Association. This organization supervised the two thousand or so Chinese laundries in Greater New York, each of which paid an annual fee for services that included mediation and translation when it was necessary to deal with American authorities.

The Laundry Association's powers were considerable and beneficial. It granted licenses to the laundries; new laundries had to register with it, and any transfer of business had to be approved. By so limiting competition, the Association decreased the danger of a hand laundry's being driven out by price cutting. And by overseeing transfers, and also sometimes making financing available, it assisted laborers eventually to become owners.

The basement and first floor of #16 were also central to the Chinese community. The basement held a gambling establishment. (But for the language barrier, the Chinese might as easily have patronized Irish gambling parlors in the saloons on Pell and Doyers streets.)

The Chinese love of gambling is well known. Nevertheless, some scholars who find the statement invidious explain that "love of gambling" must be viewed in the unique context of Chinatown. With the community's scarcity of recreational opportunities, with employers who encouraged gambling and sometimes even organized games to recoup part of the wages they'd paid out, and with the paucity of women, gambling is thereby justified—as if justification were needed in a country passionately addicted to lottery tickets, river boats, and the casinos of Las Vegas and Atlantic City—as a substitute for a normal home life.

The first floor held a joss house, a place of worship. Here a statue of the black-faced Kwan Goon sat on a raised throne of carved wood. Before him, on an altar, were utensils for sacrifice, bronze urns holding incense, and joss sticks made from perfumed punk. (Kwan Goon is not a deity in the Western sense. A character in the novel *Romance of the Three Kingdoms*, and by tradition thought to have been based on a real person, a famous general, Kwan Goon is a folk hero known for his honesty, his bravery, and his undying loyalty to his friends.)

Although the restaurants of Chinatown sought to attract tourists, most of the shops did not. This shelf-packed store, with its hand-made candles, catered to its own population in the hemmed-in community and to those Chinese who lived in the rear of the hand-laundry shops scattered throughout the City.

5

Quong Yuen Shing Grocery, 32 Mott Street

Site of the oldest remaining grocery store in Chinatown, Quong Yuen Shing was established in 1892 by a member of the Lee family. The date of the very first store is arguable. Some sources say 1872, when Wo Kee set up at 34 Mott Street.

Other sources give 1878 and a shop on Oliver Street, which, because of the unfriendliness of the neighborhood, transferred to what is now Mosco Street and later to Mott. Whatever the truth, at the turn of the century some thirty groceries catered to the inhabitants of Chinatown, and most had a Mott Street address.

Heaped outside in open bins lay a profusion of fresh vegetables of varieties then unfamiliar to New Yorkers, raised by Chinese farmers on Long Island and in New Jersey. Even today, when most of the bok choy, ginger, bitter melon, snow peas, and Chinese broccoli come from Florida, there are still farms near Englishtown, New Jersey, that provision Chinatown's groceries, as they have for a century.

The groceries also sold dry goods, kitchenware, and medicines either made in the store or imported from China. Behind long wooden counters on narrow shelves sat small packages of roots and herbs wrapped in paper. On the floors stood barrels, boxes, and jars of all sizes.

Patronized by customers who came from villages closest to the shopkeeper's area of origin and who therefore spoke the same Cantonese dialect (of which there are some three hundred), the groceries served multiple purposes. The counter clerks very likely read aloud letters received– the shops also served as mail drops–and wrote letters home for their largely illiterate customers. News could be shared. Social contacts could be enjoyed. In such ways, these groceries resembled the country stores of small-town and rural America.

Unlike the proprietors of country stores, however, the owners of Chinese groceries—wealthy and well connected—usually occupied top leadership positions in their clan and village associations. As a group, they were the most powerful force in Chinatown, not least because they could provide jobs and extend loans to relatives and newcomers alike.

Beginning in 1801, the stone-towered Church of the Transfiguration has consecutively served immigrants of German, Irish, Italian, and now Chinese heritage.

6 | Church of the Transfiguration, 29 Mott Street

The Roman Catholic Church of the Transfiguration [see also Irish stop #10 and Italian stop #2] is overwhelmingly Chinese today, operating an elementary school for Chinese children (most of whom are Buddhists) and offering English-language classes and job-training programs for adults. The Chinese Service Center around the corner on Mosco Street is also run by Transfiguration.

The church was originally built for English Lutherans who, by 1853, had moved away and sold the building to an Irish congregation of Roman Catholics. But in selling the building, the Lutherans did not necessarily disappear from the neighborhood. Throughout the Lower East Side, Protestants tended to return as missionaries. Their proselytizing had little effect on the Irish but met with considerable success among the Italians; by 1913, forty-two Protestant churches or missions in the City were operating in the Italian language. Jews were as resistant as the Irish. No matter. The Catholic hierarchy, all of whom were Irish, and Jewish leaders protested fiercely. So the missions turned their focus on people they viewed as heathen. Here again conversions were numerically few. But later, when the Chinese community began to expand and require family services that bachelor-society Chinatown was ill prepared to supply, the Protestant missions—and this Roman Catholic church—grew increasingly successful in attracting Chinese members.

The fact that Transfiguration could exist for generations after most of the Irish and Italians had moved away demonstrates the strength of their communities and their attachment to this church. But that it existed for so long with little or no Chinese participation may also be indicative of interethnic tensions.

With one resident doctor practicing Western medicine, the Chinese Hospital on Park (now Mosco) Street served those few in the community sufficiently acculturated to turn their backs on—or, more likely, add to—the tried-and-true herbal medicines and acupuncture of their homeland.

7 | Hospital, 105 Mosco Street

On this site—initially called Park Street and, in the 1970s, renamed for an Italian-American politician—stood the first hospital in the City to treat Chinese patients. We can assume that the treatments offered combined Chinese and Western medicine.

But of course the Chinese had recourse to medical attention in their own language before the establishment of this hospital. An herbal doctor probably arrived with the first group of laborers.

115

Rather than a full-time professional, he would most likely have been a person who, somewhere along the line—perhaps from his father, perhaps from formal study—had picked up experience with herbal medicines. Word of mouth would have brought the immigrant community to him for treatment.

Herbalists still practice in Chinatown today, and for the same reasons—the presence of a new community of immigrants, unable to afford, and possibly not willing to trust, Western medical treatment. As one of the newcomers told a *New York Times* reporter, "What matters is if they can cure you. They don't need a license to be able to cure people. I stay with herbalist."

Within the Chinese hospital, a doctor takes the pulse of a laborer.

8 Joss Houses, 15 and 20 Mott Street

At these locations stood two more of Chinatown's many, and generally priestless, joss houses—so many that it has been suggested that they served more to attract tourists seeking the "mysterious Orient" than to satisfy Chinese religious needs.

Unlike Western religions, which are strongly site specific—under normal circumstances, worship involves an ordained leader and a congregation—much of Chinese religion can be

A well-dressed visitor to a joss house face to face with an attendant responsible for keeping incense sticks burning for the synthetic thrills of the tourist.

practiced anywhere an adherent can meditate or pray. And since much observance deals with paying honor to ancestors, shrines need not be large or fixed in one location. A shrine beside a cot, in the back room of a laundry, or beside the stove in a restaurant will suffice.

Like the joss house on the first floor of 16 Mott Street [see stop #4], these temples probably included a statue of Kwang Goon. As the protector of travelers—and certainly the immigrants were that—he held a particular attraction for overseas communities. But his appearance in these temples did not mean that no other deities were present.

Whether at these addresses or elsewhere—there were many, usually short-lived, popping up and disappearing, depending on the times—joss houses normally incorporated ancestor worship along with various proportions of Confucian, Taoist, Buddhist, Islamic, and even Christian influences. Obscuring the value of such ecumenical breadth, a 1955 report for the National Conference of the Chinese Christian Conference blandly concluded, "there [is] tolerance for different religious points of view."

No joss house remains in contemporary Chinatown. Two explanations seem persuasive: real estate values have risen and numerous Christian churches in the area, many led by Chinese ministers, always resented their existence. 117

Although almost all of them were descended from families in Canton, a southern province, the Chinese in New York held no regional prejudice when it came to the Japanese invasion of the north. Their country was again being victimized, and in 1937 Chinatown followed the grim news as it was posted on bulletin boards such as this.

9 | ## Corner of Mott and Pell Streets

Here was the center of Old Chinatown. Until the first daily newspaper to be regularly published appeared in 1915, a bulletin board and an "electric pillar" (probably a public-address system) at this corner provided information to the news-hungry residents of the community. During the 1930s and 1940s, when China was fighting the Japanese, the corner also became the place to distribute leaflets, to hold rallies, and to collect contributions to patriotic organizations and to the war effort itself.

Apart from the daily paper, there were many less frequently published newspapers, most notably the *Chinese Reform News* [see stop #3]. They advocated a variety of political views, expressing the beliefs of whatever business or family association sponsored them. But as with other immigrant groups on the Lower East Side, many Chinese were illiterate. News was best communicated in the early days by word of mouth.

Those early Chinese with the time or desire to learn to read their own language could have availed themselves of formal tutors located through the associations and the CCBA. If they wanted to learn English, Christian organizations like the Forsyth Mission (later The Church of All Nations) held classes.

Lee Family Association, 41 Mott Street

The surname Lee (together with Moy and Ng) formed the largest surname group in the community. And given the number of Lees, their long history in China, and their ability to organize, their association was (and is) also among the most influential. A shared surname is even more important than a shared place of origin because no matter what their geographical origins, people with the same surname will often form an association, meet to socialize, and set up a rotating credit system among themselves.

In the six-story building at #41, into which the Lee Association moved in 1975 (the marble facing was applied the next year), there is a family ancestral hall, a conference room, a reading area, game rooms, and a loan association. If registered with the association, any Lee, and anyone directly related to a Lee by blood, could (and can) apply for a loan for personal or business purposes. But receiving the loan depended on the person's long-standing relationship to the organization and his known reliability.

Through what eventually amounted to their own private savings and loan bank, members of the Lee Association came to own a number of groceries and considerable real estate along Mott Street between Bayard and Chatham Square.

This school on Mott Street used hymnals and the Bible to teach English to adults. Founded by Methodists, it was funded by members of various denominations, all eager to instruct the "heathen" in Christianity.

11 | Lein Chen and Ning Yung Associations, 47 Mott Street

This gracious old building houses the two most powerful district associations in Chinatown—Ning Yung and Lein Chen. Until as late as 1960, 60 percent of Chinatown's residents came from the Toishen district of Guangdong Province—which Westerners simplify into Canton. They automatically were members of the Ning Yung Association. Everyone else—mainly from nearby areas—belonged to Lein Chen.

Early models of such associations date back as far as twenty or twenty-five generations in certain areas of China. The district associations, as they developed overseas, began to diverge from the models when their members faced new situations and developed new interests. Together with family associations, these two district associations regulated businesses and mediated disputes within groups. The CCBA was more concerned with intergroup rivalries.

12 | Tai Pei Liquor Store, 53 Mott Street

Today the shop is Mark's Wine and Liquor, but until the 1930s, the original store at this location marked the northern border of Chinatown. Walking north from this point today shows the extent and vitality of the current ethnic Chinese immigration, and close observation reveals that the sweatshop remains the grim source of immigrant wages.

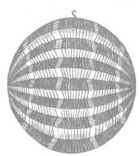

13 | Pell Street

The buildings on Pell Street look today, and are lived in today, much as they were in the nineteenth century, when the neighborhood was largely Irish with an admixture of Jews and Italians. In small, dingy railroad flats above the shops, men shared space with their male relatives, family friends, or fellow villagers. It was common for as many as a dozen men to live in a single apartment, filled wall to wall with beds—wooden planks set on sawhorses—each occupied by three persons in successive eight-hour shifts.

The English lettering on the banner vividly demonstrates that the merchants of Chinatown, with trading partners outside the boundaries of the community, were also contributing to the economy of the nation.

14 | Hip Sing Tong, 16 Pell Street

Tongs (the word means "halls"), the secret fraternal associations of Chinatown, originated in Taiwan and Fujian as "triads" back in the eighteenth century. Known as the Heaven and Earth Society, the first triads, which bound their members together through religious ritual and oaths of allegiance, were a political force that sought to unseat the Manchus (Qing dynasty). The inability of the Qing dynasty to deal with the imperialist powers, and to protect the country

14

cont.

against the regional rivalry between Russia and Japan, strongly contributed to disillusionment with the existing government. Ethnic differences also underlay this sense of Manchu illegitimacy.

According to Jonathan Spence, the distinguished contemporary historian of modern China, by the 1830s triad lodges, whose first members were sailors and poor city dwellers (including women!), also began to attract "numerous peasant recruits, perhaps because in south China, where powerful lineages often controlled entire villages, the triads offered an alternative form of protection and an organizational focus to those living on the edge of destitution."

The triads' descendants, the tongs of Chinatown—which were (and remain) open to anyone (but probably no longer to women), regardless of surname or place of origin—first appeared in the early 1880s. They functioned to protect their members' jobs or business interests. Over the years, and not unlike Italian village associations that sometimes fed into the Camorra and the Mafia, the tongs evolved into criminal organizations controlling drugs, prostitution, gambling, and loan-sharking. Their methods included extortion and physical violence; thus the respectable surname and district associations were (and are) hard put to compete against them.

Each tong had its own sphere of influence within which it had exclusive rights to criminal operations. Inside the Hip Sing headquarters—within all tong quarters—were gambling halls offering mahjong, fan-tan (in which the players bet on the number of beans shaken out of a cup), pai gow (a form of poker played with dominoes), and lottery to a population whose lives otherwise held little amusement. With its traditional rival, the On Leong tong, it fought sporadically for more than four decades about which one was to oversee local gambling and opium trafficking. And their dead continued to pile up on Doyers Street [see stop #15].

The tongs remain, and they continue to participate in CCBA politics. Hip Sing is the largest and most powerful, although now that liberalized immigration laws and a geographically extended Chinatown allow admittance to Chinese from areas other than Guangdong Province, Hip Sing and the other "native" tongs are facing competition, sometimes armed and bloody, from a Fujianese tong.

15 Doyers Street

In the early years, Doyers was a dead-end alley, its angled length blocked by a building at the corner of Pell Street. At the height of the tong war in the 1920s, Doyers became known as Dead Men's (or Bloody) Alley. There was no escape if one were chased into it by rival tong members.

Tong wars were not simply the stuff of headline exaggerations in the yellow press. When territorial interests could no longer be resolved peacefully—when, for example, the Chinese population was growing rapidly as a result of migration from West Coast communities in the 1920s—forces within Chinatown hired "hatchetmen," unemployed members of tongs, to fight the conflicts to a bloody resolution.

The issue of who won and who lost was not always clear even to the participants. The fact was that with little possibility of moving out of the area—lack of resources, impermeable immigrant groups surrounding them, and the prejudices held by outside communities—most Chinese immigrants had only the four to five blocks of Old Chinatown as a place to establish businesses. Thus, tensions were a permanent fact of life as groups vied for the same real estate and resources. And the old wars didn't stop until the 1930s, when American authorities threatened to deport the tongs' leaders.

16 The Chinese Opera House, 5-7 Doyers Street

Several local theaters performed Cantonese opera during the 1890s. The one at this location—it was in the basement of a lodging house—had seats for five hundred people and gave performances at six o'clock every evening. The Great China Theater on the Bowery presented operas every evening at nine.

Cantonese opera, like the more familiar Beijing opera, employs instruments found in Western orchestras—violin, viola, and bass—but because the modal music produced requires for its appreciation a more sophisticated ear than most Western auditors had in the years when tickets were affordable, performances were almost never attended by "uptown" tourists. Scenery, costumes, and makeup also differ from those of Beijing. The actors' faces, because they are not heavily painted, show considerable expression. This reduction of the extreme stylization found in Beijing opera is thought to be the result of cultural adaptation by southern Chinese exposed to American dramatic realism.

Popular as the operas were, the theater at #5-7 closed when a City ordinance (possibly selectively applied) prohibited it from staying open on Sundays, the one day most Chinese had free. Its location was taken by the Rescue Society, established by an ex-convict named Tom Noonan, who dedicated himself to easing the lives of Bowery derelicts, very few of whom were Chinese.

17 The Bowery Along Chatham Square

For a description of the Bowery as the elegant center of Lower East Side entertainment, see German stop #6. But all things change. By the time the Chinese arrived in force, the Bowery had already begun to degenerate, and its name turned into a generic label for areas populated by drunks and the homeless seeking flophouses in which to spend the night.

But the Bowery also figures in Chinatown's history. In addition to the Cantonese opera that played there, there was Miss Campbell's Presbyterian Mission. Miss Campbell was famous for saving and reforming prostitutes, among them Chinese girls who had been smuggled in by tongs.

Many of the girls had been sold to the tongs by impoverished parents; others had been kidnapped when female-scarce Chinatowns, here and elsewhere in the country, became recognized as lucrative markets for women. It should go without saying that had United States law been different—had Chinese women not been legally excluded—there would have been little need for this trade. As it was, over half of the all too few married couples in Chinatown were interracial, with most of the women being Irish.

At #22 is the oldest Chinese coffee shop. Established in the 1930s as the Bamboo Garden, it remains popular with the working class. Along with coffee, steamed bread, rice cakes, dumplings, and wonton soup, it serves tea—tea such as the inhabitants of Old Chinatown would have looked on with amazement: it's made with tea bags and served with milk. Like chop suey, such a desecration is not native to New York's original Chinese population, nor was it adapted from Western tradition; it comes from Hong Kong.

18 | Funeral Parlors, 26 and 36 Mulberry Street

The first undertaker to be used by the community
—he was not Chinese—was located at 2 Mulberry Street. But in the 1930s the Chinese began
to run their own highly profitable establishments.
Neither of these two Chinese funeral parlors on
Mulberry Street is particularly old. The building
at #36 that houses Ng Fook (founded in 1976)
was originally a bank and then an Italian funeral
parlor. Wah Wing at #26 was established in 1955.

At the more impressive funerals, Italian brass
bands group on the sidewalk and play tunes
familiar to Western ears. Speculation has it that
the bands may serve a Chinese purpose by sym-
bolically clearing the area of ill spirits, much as
fire crackers and percussive instruments do at
New Year's celebrations. The explanation does
not exclude the possibility that families simply
like the sound.

From these funeral parlors, most of the coffins
are taken to Evergreen Cemetery in Brooklyn,
where an entire foothill is now crowded with
Chinese tombstones. The section was purchased
in the 1920s by a group of associations in order
that Chinatown's residents who either couldn't
afford to have their bones shipped home to their
ancestral villages (a very expensive transaction
on which handlers, if they weren't family members, made a fortune) or who no longer thought
it necessary would have a place to be buried.

The continuation of burials in America suggests
a geographic reorientation. Most members of
the Chinese community no longer thought to
earn money and return to their villages; in fact,
about half of all who had come prior to 1930—
nationwide about four hundred thousand—
chose to remain here. Then, with the dropping
of restrictions against Asian immigration and
the chance to live as human beings—as members of families—New York's Chinese were at

last permitted to face the difficulties of America on an equal footing with the other "foreigners" who had built new lives in this neighborhood of immigrants.

EPILOGUE

Where are they now, the descendants of the Chinese of the Lower East Side? Many, now prosperous, still own businesses in the neighborhood but live elsewhere—Queens and Westchester County, for example. Many more are professionals—doctors, university professors, architects, scientists–and live wherever their work calls them. But few have forgotten how difficult it was, or how long it took, for the Chinese to be accepted as "real" Americans. Some doubt that it has happened even yet.

Six Tours of the **Lower East Side**

S
L, M101,102

① E. 12TH

Second Ave

First Ave

St. Mark's Place

TOMPKINS SQUARE PARK

Avenue A

Avenue B

Houston

Norfolk

Suffolk

Stanton

Rivington

Chrystie

Sara Delano Roosevelt Park

Eldridge

Allen

Orchard

Ludlow

J,M,Z,F,M9,14,15,B39

⑮
⑯
S Delancey   Williamsburg Bridge

Essex

Broome

Broome

Mott

Bowery

Forsyth

S

⑨

Grand

⑩

Hester

⑧

Montgomery

⑪
S ⑤
⑦

Canal

⑫
⑥

Clinton

Jefferson

⑬
④
②
③

Rutgers

Bayard

Division

East Broadway

Henry

Pike

Manhattan Bridge

Chatham Square

Market

Water

Catherine

⑭
Oliver

St. James Pl

James St

Eastern European Jewish Heritage

Were one to trace the immigration of Jews to Manhattan Island, the starting date would be September 1654, with the arrival of twenty-three Sephardic Jewish refugees who had sailed to New Amsterdam from Brazil. Our concern, however, largely limited to the late nineteenth and early twentieth centuries, focuses primarily on the Eastern European, Yiddish-speaking Jews who flooded the Lower East Side beginning in the 1880s. (The earlier-arriving German Jews are discussed in the German Heritage chapter.)

Very few people of any nationality or religion emigrate from their native lands because their lives lack adventure. They leave because the soil they cultivate is exhausted; because, over generations, the land has been so subdivided that what is left to them is insufficient for a livelihood; because there is no longer a niche for them in a changing economy; because wars, epidemics, and famines destroy hope;

because governments make them targets of repression. Those are the "pushes" that convince people to leave. The "pull" is their hope of improving their lives in another land.

Eastern European Jews didn't farm; they were not permitted to own land. But the disruptions in the agricultural economy across all of Europe constricted their role as middlemen and as small artisans. And as dwellers in the *shtetls* (villages) in the Pale of Settlement that stretched across Poland, Ukraine, and Byelorussia, few were able to take up the factory jobs the Industrial Revolution was creating in the cities. Finally, notoriously, not only were they afflicted by the tsarist terms of military service—by this time reduced from twenty-five to sixteen years, during which stretch it was impossible for a conscript to eat or worship as a Jew—but they were also the direct object of pogroms, those governmentally encouraged massacres that made it impossible to live as a Jew. At the other extreme, America was thought of as the Golden Land.

The number of Eastern European Jews in the United States by 1880 is estimated at fifty thousand. In the following ten years, during which tsarist Russia took measures leading to their economic and cultural stagnation, such as restrictions on their admission to universities, still more Jews—some one hundred seventy million of them—fled from Russian-ruled lands. In each succeeding year, the numbers increased. In the 1890s, the Jews of Romania joined the modern exodus; three hundred thousand in that decade. Another one and a half million arrived between 1900 and 1917.

Unlike the Chinese and the Italians, the Jews had every intention of remaining in America. And it often must have seemed as if every last one of them meant to take root in the Lower East Side.

The German Jews—who had arrived decades earlier and who feared that their own acceptance in the country would be jeopardized by their less educated, less sophisticated coreligionists from Eastern Europe—were appalled from the very beginning by this "foreign" migration. Yet in the hope of preventing the doors of immigration from shutting, they tried to minimize the impact of the flood. Through philanthropies, they worked to ameliorate the plight of the immigrants, to Americanize them, to advance them, and in a few instances to disperse them. The philanthropist Jacob Schiff, for example, sponsored the Galveston Movement. By directing boatloads of immigrants away from the port of New York with offers of jobs in "outlandish" locations ranging from Oklahoma to the Dakotas and Oregon, the Schiff plan was responsible for some ten thousand Jews disembarking in Galveston, Texas, between 1907 and 1914.

Schiff was not entirely off-base, however. Not a few Jews had already settled in the western states and were doing well. The notorious Dodge City, for instance, had a Jewish mayor at one point in the nineteenth century, and a Jewish councilman in Dodge was the person who chose Wyatt Earp to be the town's sheriff.

But if Schiff had it in mind to turn Jews into farmers, he was, with few exceptions, dramatically unsuccessful. In overwhelming numbers, the Eastern European Jews preferred the major cities of the East Coast—Boston, Philadelphia, Baltimore; best of all, New York. The Lower East Side, home to Irish and Germans, now absorbed Jews, Jews, and more Jews. It became the most densely inhabited area in the Western world.

Who were these city-loving immigrants? Mostly they had been born in lands that are today Russia, Poland, Ukraine, Belarus, Lithuania, and Romania. They tended to be younger than previous immigrant groups. Because they meant to stay, they mostly came in families.

In general, those arriving in the early 1880s or before were neither deeply religious nor strongly political. The most Orthodox, if they chose emigration, preferred the Holy Land. The most political—the Bundists—preferred to fight the good fight at home.

As time passed, the nature (though not the number) of emigrating Jews changed. As pogrom followed pogrom, many of the Orthodox fled for their lives. When the Revolution of 1905 failed, many of the Bundists—strong secularists who combined socialism with Jewish nationalism—left Russia either because they gave up hope of reforming the government or because remaining meant literal imprisonment. Still others, the intellectuals, came to escape oppression and to create a new world for their people.

The intellectuals held "advanced" views: in place of religion as the cement holding Jews together, they promoted socialism as the binding principle between peoples of all nations. They invested their language—Yiddish—with new value, and sometimes they had to learn

Yiddish in order to do so. It became for them something more than *mama-loshen* (mother's tongue); they used it now as a language in which to think worldly thoughts, to write secular literature, and to reach and influence the masses.

The later they came, the more education and work skills they possessed. But despite the assumption that Jews immediately went into commerce, only about a fourth did. And this commerce was often very small-time—nothing grander than peddling. The 10 percent who became peddlers sold everything from peacock feathers and dyed grasses to celluloid collar buttons, potatoes, and secondhand coats, all either from pushcarts lined up on the streets of the Lower East Side or from packs they carried into the hinterlands. Those having appropriate abilities painted apartments, baked bread, or opened delicatessens and corner "candy" stores. And because money was to be made, some also opened gambling houses and brothels. Most, however, toiled at home and in factories in the garment industry, whose center was New York.

Together, the immigrants formed a noisy, intensely crowded, and fractious community that in one way was totally different from the *shtetls* and ghettos from which they had come. Here they lived in five- and six-story tenements: three rooms without a view. In other ways, the Lower East Side almost precisely resembled their old world: it was mostly poor and it was wholly Jewish.

Actor-impresario Jacob Adler's Grand Street Theatre in 1904 promises yet another performance of *The Jewish King Lear,* all the more tragic to its Yiddish-speaking audiences because the conflict between patriarch and children reflected the division between their own European and American generations.

Eastern European Jewish Tour

1 | **Yiddish Art Theater, Southwest Corner of Second Avenue and 12th Street**

This present-day movie house with its neo-Moorish interior was built in 1926 for Maurice Schwartz's Yiddish Art Theater. The company earned the "art" in its name honestly. Founded in 1918 at the old Irving Place Theater, Schwartz's theater offered in its lifetime (it folded in 1950) plays by living European writers such as George Bernard Shaw and Artur Schnitzler, by classical playwrights such as Molière, and by almost all the Yiddish playwrights of merit. But in spite of (or because of?) Schwartz's remarkable breadth and energy as director, the productions were uneven. In his *World of Our Fathers,* Irving

Howe says, "Schwartz yoked together all the conflicting impulses of Yiddish theatre and made of them an exuberant tension, sometimes brilliant, sometimes absurd."

On the other hand, even at their absurdist worst, the quality of Schwartz's productions had to have been a far cry from that of the theatricals produced in the 1880s during the earliest years of Yiddish theater on the Lower East Side. The very first play—an operetta with a cast that included the young Boris Thomashefsky—would seem to have been staged in the *Neue Turnhalle* [see German stop #9] on East Fourth Street. The production was disapproved of by both Orthodox and German Jews, the one thinking it sacrilegious, the other viewing it as uncultured.

But opposition could not quench the thirst of actors and directors, or of immigrant audiences who wanted some lightening of their lives and some staged exploration of their experiences in both the new and old worlds. "From start to finish," Irving Howe tells us, "the theatre would be their great cultural passion."

Initially, the theaters were grouped on Grand Street. The Grand Theater, on the southwest corner of Grand and Chrystie streets (a site that now lies within Sara Delano Roosevelt Park), was home to Jacob Adler and his talented acting family. Thomashevsky's first theater was on Grand Street and the Bowery. By the turn of the century, these and other Grand Street theaters presented some eleven hundred performances annually for an audience estimated at two million.

From Grand Street the Yiddish "Broadway" moved up to Second Avenue between Houston and 14th streets, where its productions and actors—some of whom, most famously Paul Muni, went on to distinguished Broadway and Hollywood careers—were admired by the most sophisticated of New York's theater critics. Today, a few plays are still produced in Yiddish for loyal audiences, but not at these theaters and not for the crowds who once filled their seats.

Preliminary to any strike, a union must swell its ranks. This appeal, calling a mass meeting for a Sabbath evening, proves that Jewish labor leaders chose to place social action above religious observance.

2 Tailors' Union, 165 East Broadway

On the eve of Yom Kippur in 1884, a group of Russian and Polish Jews came together on the top floor of this building in an early effort at unionization. They formed the Tailors' Union. Abraham Cahan, editor of the *Forward* [see stop #3], served as speaker and discussion guide.

The following day, a group of pressers held their own meeting. Here too the talk was of a strike. The upshot was the first general strike in the men's clothing industry, during which the tailors succeeded in organizing the majority of piece-work shops—five thousand men working as operators, basters, finishers, pressers, and bushlers. This union eventually failed, but the need for unions did not. In his autobiography, the journalist Roy Stannard Baker told why.

> *[My 1904 article for* McClure's*] concerned the effort of a number of farsighted and idealistic labor leaders to organize the most poverty-stricken, unrecognized and undefended people in the country—masses of new immigrants who spoke little or no English, who were remorselessly exploited and cheated at every turn. They were the Russian Jews of the slums of New York, and Southern Italians, and Poles and Portuguese and Greeks who were workers in the garment*

industries....Not one of the articles I wrote at that time more deeply aroused my interest and sympathy.

New York was the center of the nation's vast garment industry. At the beginning of the century, close to a million people toiled at its various tasks. And how those million labored! The norm was sixty-five hours a week; during the height of the season, seventy-five. Wages were equally grim, averaging between four and twelve dollars a week, which translates into five and sixteen cents an hour. Female wages were lower—for the same work week, women earned an average ranging between three and nine dollars. What wonder that the garment workers—about 75 percent Jewish and 15 percent Italian at the beginning of the century—thought militantly about issues of capital and labor. Despite long-standing ideological conflicts—activists divided into anarchists, syndicalists, communists, socialists of varying stripes, and "simple" trade unionists, each feuding with the others and among

The "union" of Union Square commemorates neither labor unions nor the northern side of the Civil War; the square was formed and named in 1831. But its broad surrounding streets made it ideal for labor demonstrations. Carrying banners reading "Agitate, Educate, Organize," "Abolish Convict Labor," and "The True Remedy—Organization & the Ballot," workers in 1882 march in support of the eight-hour day and increased union membership.

137

2

cont.

themselves—the workers came together often enough between 1909 and 1914 to stage a number of major strikes.

Perhaps the most memorable—variously celebrated as the "Great Revolt" or the "Uprising of the Twenty Thousand"—began with workers in the shirtwaist factories, 80 percent of whom were young Jewish women. In particular, it began with almost a thousand women who worked for the Triangle Shirtwaist factory [see Italian stop #13]. Backed by the International Ladies Garment Workers and the United Hebrew Trades and supported by well-to-do women, mostly Protestants, who had recently formed the New York Women's Trade Union League, the Triangle workers took to the streets in September 1909. For five weeks they and the ladies of the Trade Union League endured threats, maulings, and arrests—to no avail. The bosses remained adamant.

When finally the workers grew discouraged, a mass meeting was called at Cooper Union [see African stop #3]. The speakers included Meyer London (a socialist soon to be elected congressman for the Lower East Side), the labor organizer and Bundist, Morris Hillquit, and Samuel Gompers, head of the American Federation of Labor [see German stop #13]. These men may or may not have been persuasive, but it was Clara Lemlich, a teenage unionist speaking in Yiddish, who won the day:

> *[The bosses] yell at the girls and "call them down" even worse than I imagine the Negro slaves were in the South. There are no dressing rooms for the girls in the shops...no place to hang a hat where it will not be spoiled by the end of the day. We're human, all of us girls, and we're young. We like new hats as well as any other young women. Why shouldn't we? And if one of us gets a new one, even if it hasn't cost more than 50 cents,*

that means that we have gone for weeks on two-cent lunches—dry cake and nothing else.

* * *

I am a working girl, one of those who are on strike. I am tired of listening to speakers who talk in general terms. What we are here for is to decide whether we shall or shall not strike. I offer a resolution that a general strike be declared now.

The audience rose as one, yelling, cheering. The general strike was on. Over twenty thousand women, out of a total workforce of thirty-two thousand in the shirtwaist factories, struck some six hundred shops. The men followed later: sixty-five thousand cloakmakers in a general strike in 1910; nine thousand furriers, women among them, in 1912; and a general strike of men's clothing workers in a general strike in 1913–14.

These actions were by no means the end of labor strife in the garment industry, but among other concessions the strikes brought ten paid holidays a year, a fifty-hour week with time and a half for overtime, *and* a continuation of the pay differential between the sexes. Men at the bottom of the pay scale normally earned more than the highest-paid women, and the best jobs went only to men. It was not information women sought when they asked, "So, what else is new?"

The election day issue of the *Forward* graphically promotes the socialist Eugene V. Debs against the Democrats' William Jennings Bryan and the eventual winner, William Howard Taft. Although Debs ran for every presidential election between 1900 and 1920, he is infrequently remembered, even by those who listen to radio station WEVD, whose call letters were chosen in his honor.

3 | Jewish Daily Forward Building, 173 East Broadway

This ten-story building, completed in 1912, was once home to *Forverts*, the most widely read Yiddish newspaper in the world. Founded in 1897, it was masterfully edited from 1902 to 1951 by Abraham Cahan, an immigrant from Vilna (now Vilnius), the "Jerusalem of the North."

The newspaper was culturally Jewish but so nonreligious that it didn't even bother to print information about holy days or synagogue events. It can be best described as socialist "in persuasion." As Cahan put it, "The Forward is the working men's organ in their every righteous fight against their oppressors; this struggle is the body of our movement. But its soul is the liberation of mankind—justice, humanity, fraternity—in brief, honest common sense and horse sense." In effect this declaration meant that Cahan felt free not to hew to the Socialist Party line when he thought it misguided, which would be whenever theoretical concerns blotted out practical needs.

Forverts published much the same news and scandal that appeared in the English-language press, but it also contained popularized articles on science, serious literature (written in or translated into Yiddish), and, beginning in 1921, daily lessons in English. Its most memorable feature was the Bintel Brief (Bundle of Letters) through which readers could ask for and receive advice on subjects ranging from love to landlords.

Today, with the enormous expansion of ethnic Chinese immigration into the Lower East Side, the building is tenanted by the New York Ling Liang Church, and signs drawn in Chinese characters conceal the lobby's original medallions picturing Bakunin, Kropotkin, Marx, and Lenin.

Similarly, the former Garden Cafeteria (East Broadway and Rutgers Street)—a kosher eatery that brewed tea for the likes of Samuel Gompers [see German stop #13], Leon Trotsky, and I. B. Singer, the *Forward* writer awarded the Nobel Prize for Literature in 1978—is now the site of a Chinese restaurant.

Above the restaurant, on the second floor, are rooms where Emma Goldman and her then lover, Alexander Berkman, discussed the formation of the American Communist Party.

4 Seward Park, East Broadway

On this site across from the *Jewish Daily Forward* building is a three-acre park named for Lincoln's secretary of state. Set out in 1901, its space was created by razing three blocks' worth of decayed tenement buildings and replacing them with the first urban playground to be built in the City. Jacob Riis, the Danish immigrant journalist and photographer, whose articles again and again drew the City fathers' attention to the appalling nature of slum life, was among those who, for seven long years, fought for the playground. "Neither stupidity, spite, nor cold-blooded neglect will be able much longer to cheat the child out of his rights," he wrote in

4

cont.

The Battle with the Slums. "The playground is here to wrestle with the gangs for the boy, and it will win."

There was, however, an unforseen consequence. Whenever tenement buildings were demolished and no new buildings erected, the population density of the neighborhood soared.

Men and boys, and perhaps a woman or two in the rear, crowded into the reading room of the Seward Park branch of the New York Public Library.

5

Seward Park Branch of the New York Public Library, 192 East Broadway

Another library built with funds left by Andrew Carnegie, Seward Park (1909) is said to have been the most heavily used branch in the system from the 1920s to the 1940s—a plausible claim given that it was open eighteen hours a day, from 6 A.M. to 1 A.M., six days a week.

The need for such hours is marked by two constants and a change: What remains constant is that tenement apartments—small, crowded, and noisy—were not and are not conducive to study. And few families living in them have ever had money to expend on the serious student's necessary reference books. The change, however, is generally overlooked. Although starting in the

1920s, the children of Eastern European immigrants began to use the schools en masse and
were responsible for the legendary flourishing
of scholarship that produced Nobel Prize-winning
men and women who had been graduated from
tuition-free City and Hunter colleges, Selma
Berrol, a historian who examined the records,
tells us that in the early years of Eastern
European immigration, Jewish children were
not the ardent scholars they are thought to have
been. In 1911, for example, only 16 percent of
them remained in school to the eighth grade—a
good percentage for a poor community, but far
smaller than is often imagined. But then it is not
often imagined—or imaginable—that once over
sixty thousand Jewish and Italian children on
the Lower East Side toiled in home sweatshops.
"Many of this immense host," wrote the poet
Edwin Markham in the January 1907 issue of
Cosmopolitan Magazine, "will never sit on a
school bench. Is it not a cruel civilization that
allows little hearts and shoulders to strain under
these grown-up responsibilities, while in the
same city a pet cur is jeweled and pampered
and aired on a fine lady's velvet lap on the
beautiful boulevards?"

Beyond the need to help support their families,
the children's dropping out—and their parents'
willingness to permit it—was also prompted by
Julia Richman, the first Jew and first woman to be
appointed as district superintendent of schools.
This fiercely single-minded graduate of "the
Normal" (later Hunter College) was as unpopular
a figure as ever came to "do good" on the Lower
East Side. Her stern German-Jewish notion of
Americanizing the children involved shaming and
berating them, and making it clear that their
Yiddish-speaking parents were inferior beings.

For those who completed grammar school, the
two day high schools on the Lower East Side—
Stuyvesant (1904) for boys, Washington Irving
(1913) for girls—were vocational, preparing students to enter the job market as skilled artisans.
Skilled *and* well educated. A member of

5

cont.

Washington Irving's first graduating class, the playwright Bella Spewack evidences in *Streets*, her memoir of growing up in the neighborhood's slums, that she studied Shakespeare and the best-known of the nineteenth-century poets in its classrooms. The still more academic high schools, those leading most directly to admission to CCNY and the Normal, were sited elsewhere, and until the 1920s such Jews as attended were primarily of German origin.

Women and men from youth to maturity studying English at the Educational Alliance. However difficult they found it, English—essential for citizenship—was also indispensable to those who sought jobs beyond the confines of the Lower East Side.

6

Educational Alliance, 197 East Broadway

Although the passion of Eastern European Jews for secular education has been exaggerated, there is little question that their first- and second-generation children attended settlement houses with eagerness. Mothers were generally less enthusiastic because the classes promoted American ways of infant care, child-rearing, and cooking. The implied message about Old Country practices was more than insulting; it was hurtful. English-language classes to prepare for citizenship, on the other hand—they were fine, for those parents who had the time. They did not have to abandon their own language, merely add another.

The Educational Alliance, brought about by a merger of organizations in 1889, given its current name in 1893, and still in operation at five additional locations in Manhattan, had as its specific goal to Americanize and assimilate the Eastern European immigrants. It was a notable success. Under its Harvard-educated director, the Alliance welcomed an aggregate of over two million immigrants in just its first eight years. Its attendees—and a stellar crowd they became, ranging from the philosopher Morris Raphael Cohen to the dancer Arthur Murray to artists like Mark Rothko and Ben Shahn—took classes, joined workshops, participated in clubs, and borrowed books from its Aguilar Free Library. Some also went to its summer camp.

In addition to offering a larger range of subjects than other settlement houses, and presenting lectures and events that drew vast crowds—in 1895 an art exhibit held in conjunction with the University Settlement drew 105,716 viewers— this "immigrant university" operated a legal aid bureau and, perhaps uniquely, a desertion bureau which helped locate husbands and fathers who had abandoned their families.

Desertion was a serious problem. Husbands, many of whom had preceded their families to America in order to earn enough to buy ship passage for those left behind, often held jobs that exposed them to a fast, Americanized way of life. Not infrequently they came to view the women they had wed in the Old Country—often through arranged marriages—as old-fashioned, as lacking in worldly experience, and as yoked to a religious orthodoxy they themselves were ready to abandon for the demands of the workplace and the ideals of socialism.

No less significant a cause of desertion was (and is for the City's recent immigrants as well) the shame of being unable to support a wife and children.

Most likely, the men gathered in front of the HIAS offices on East Broadway were seeking employment. Citizenship was important, as the sign implies, but jobs were crucial.

7 | Hebrew Immigrant Aid Society, 229-231 East Broadway

This location once housed two of the more lasting institutions to be launched on the Lower East Side: Young Israel and the offices of the Hebrew Immigrant Aid Society (HIAS).

HIAS was created in 1902 through a merger of three groups: the Voliner Zhitomir Aid Society, which originally helped only those Jews hailing from the Ukrainian towns of Volin and Zhitomir; the Jewish Emigrant Protective Society; and the Hebrew Sheltering House Society.

In support of an enlarged aim—to assist needy immigrants, regardless of their country of origin or their religion—HIAS sent its representatives straight to Ellis Island. Did the bewildered newcomers need a place to live? Jobs? Medical attention? Train tickets out of New York? HIAS was there to help.

In 1921, when HIAS moved to 425 Lafayette Street, it took a giant step up. Its new headquarters, described by the *AIA Guide to New York*

City as "a funky, generously scaled red brick and brownstone building considered by some to be the finest American example of *Rundbogenstil*, a German variant of Romanesque Revival," had been built between 1853 and 1881 to house John Jacob Astor's library [see the German Heritage introduction]. Into HIAS's old space moved the Young Israel Synagogue of Manhattan [see stop #13].

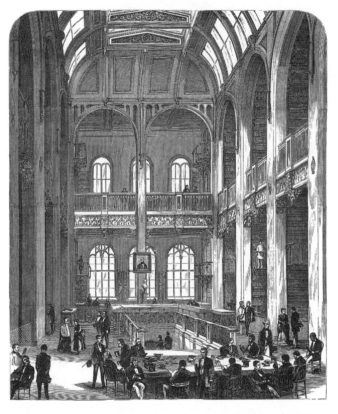

Under this dome, which originally capped John Jacob Astor's library, HIAS found its second home. It also housed YIVO, the Yiddish Research Institute, after it escaped Nazi-invaded Vilna. In 1875, when the picture was drawn, the library, open to the public, is said to have held the largest collection of books in America—one hundred fifty thousand volumes.

Lillian Wald, the Cincinnati-born nurse who took the Lower East side under her wing at the Henry Street Settlement.

8 | Henry Street Settlement, 263-267 Henry Street

The justly famous and beloved Lillian Wald (1867-1940) founded the Henry Street Settlement (originally called the Nurse's Settlement) on Rivington Street in 1893. Its second site was here on Henry Street in first one, then two, then three townhouses. The buildings are now landmarked.

Wald, a German Jew born in Cincinnati, had little interest in Americanizing her Eastern European coreligionists. As a trained nurse, her concern was for their well-being: in addition to medical care, they needed and she helped supply food and jobs. Having herself walked the streets of the Lower East Side—up Ludlow, down Hester, across Clinton; she kept records of it all—Wald, with her personal experience of tending the sick, formed the very first nonsectarian public health nursing system in the world and the first school-nurse service in the City. Still more remarkable, by 1916, her nurses—by then there were about a hundred—were making well over two hundred thousand house calls a year.

Unimaginable, even considering that to save constant climbing up tenement stairs, they reached their patients by crossing from rooftop to rooftop and descending on the ill.

Across the street, at #152, is a Buddhist temple. Prior to its conversion in 1990, the building—whose original name was translated as "House of Sages"—served as a religious and social center for retired rabbis who continued to live in the neighborhood.

9 Beth Hamedrash Hagadol (Great House of Study), 60 Norfolk Street

Built in 1850 as the Norfolk Street Baptist Church, this now-landmarked structure was purchased by Hungarian Jews in 1885. Theirs was a distinguished congregation: when eleven Orthodox congregations banded together in a call for a chief rabbi, the man selected also served as the rabbi here.

Although he spoke neither German nor English, their choice was Jacob Joseph, who had been a rabbinic judge and community preacher in Vilna. In New York he was expected to adjudicate issues of marriage and divorce for a contentious multinational clientele, as well as to reform the kosher meat industry. Both jobs were probably impossible for any rabbi to fulfill; they certainly were for the mild-mannered Rabbi Joseph.

Even though he failed at his tasks and the eleven congregations gave up the idea of a chief rabbi, Joseph himself was well regarded. At his early death in 1902, between fifty and one hundred thousand people turned out for the funeral procession as his coffin was carried from synagogue to synagogue on its way to a gravesite in Brooklyn.

9

cont.

On the route, the procession was harassed by workers, predominately Irish, from the R. H. Hoe printing plant (now the site of the Amalgamated Dwellings and Hillman Houses on Grand Street). The police egged the workers on. The antagonism went beyond differences in religion; it also resided in the now familiar question "Whose neighborhood is it anyway?" The Irish had been immigrating into the Lower East Side since the 1830s. But especially since the 1880s, their turf had been increasingly invaded by "foreigners," people who, except for their poverty and dreams, were very different from themselves. The Irish and Jews were not the first--and alas, not the last—of the ethnic groups to confront each other with fear and hostility.

When this photograph was taken, around 1900, both Hester and Orchard streets were nearly impassable. When Mayor La Guardia brought the pushcart vendors under roof at the Essex Street Market, for the first time in nearly fifty years fire engines were not delayed in reaching a conflagration.

10 | Chazzer Market, Ludlow and Hester Streets

This intersection, known as Pig Market, served as an outdoor hiring hall. Because of the seasonal nature of the garment industry—in winter it made summer clothes; in summer, winter clothes—Jewish tailors gathered here during the off seasons in the hope of picking up jobs.

Hester Street (and Orchard Street) was also famous for its pushcart market. Jacob Riis can again be relied on for documentation:

> *There is scarcely anything else [other than pork] that can be hawked from a wagon that is not to be found, and at ridiculously low prices. Bandannas and tin cups at two cents, peaches at a cent a quart, "damaged" eggs for a song....The crowds that jostle each other at the wagons and about the sidewalk shops, where a gutter plank of two ash-barrels does the duty for a counter! Pushing, struggling, babbling, and shouting in foreign tongues, a veritable Babel of confusion.*

11 | Landsmanshaft Building, 5 Ludlow Street

This L-shaped building housed, among other mutual-aid societies, the Kletzker Brotherly Aid Association, one of the hundred or more *landsmanshaftn* formed by *landslayt* (immigrants from the same town or region of the Old Country) to offer their members medical care, unemployment insurance, a community burial plot, social activities, and the comfort of a shared background. Mutual-aid societies, for all immigrant groups, were and are a natural outgrowth of being uprooted.

A few *landsmanshaftn* may also have had a less benevolent underside. In 1908, Police Commissioner Theodore Bingham, in an article for the *North American Review,* claimed that they were also centers for criminal activity. More than that, he claimed that Jews accounted for half of the City's criminals.

11

cont.

True enough. Even the head of the YMHA admitted that some 30 percent of the youngsters in correctional facilities were the children of Jewish immigrants. (The leading cause of their arrests, at least in 1909, was the pilfering of coal and wood—precisely what was required to fire up a tenement stove.)

But there was an adult underworld as well, with Jews involved in fencing stolen goods, gambling, arson, and prostitution. These activities were no secret. The Jewish community knew, just as we know but sometimes forget, that poverty produces crime no matter what the ethnic background. What most outraged and mortified the community, however, was that Bingham and reformist members of the Christian clergy were implying a specifically Jewish propensity for criminal behavior. That was not to be borne.

> *Defiled, the Jewish community now turned on itself in an agony of recrimination. Orthodox rabbis ascribed the tragedy to a flight from tradition; Socialists, to capitalistic exploitation; business leaders, to radical ideologies. Whatever the cause, all factions agreed that the symptoms had to be treated immediately.* (Howard Sachar, *A History of the Jews in America*)

A *kehillah* (community organization) under the direction of Rabbi Judah Magnes of Temple Emanu-El [see German stop #1] was formed to respond to Bingham. During the life of the *kehillah*'s "social morals" bureau, its investigator gathered information on petty and major Jewish criminals [see also stop #16] and shared its findings with the mayor, who did or did not share it with the police. In any event, by the 1920s, as Howard Sachar puts it, " 'Jews' and 'criminality' ceased to be interchangeable terms in the public vernacular."

(The building on the corner next to the Kletzker Brotherly Aid Association now houses the Tung Goon Association, a Chinese benevolent society.

When not viewed as "model" immigrants, the Chinese too are regularly attacked for "having a propensity" for criminality.)

12 Jarmulowsky's Bank, 54-58 Canal Street

This huge building, which takes up most of the block, stands as a symbol of hubris, overweening pride. Named for the sons of Sender Jarmulowsky, it opened in 1912 and was bankrupt two years later.

Jarmolowsky, who began as a peddler, started his banking career in 1873, catering primarily to Jewish immigrants who believed in saving for rainier days than they already knew. The rains came at the outbreak of World War I. At that point, depositors, now both Jewish and Italian, sought to withdraw their money. They wanted it in nice, dependable gold and silver coins—not only because they wished to send money to relatives who, they feared, could be trapped by the war in Europe but also because they lacked confidence in paper money. Some banks couldn't meet the demand. In August 1914, three banks, including Jarmulowsky's, were shut down by the superintendent of banking, and the immigrant depositors, who rightly feared they had lost all or most of their savings, rioted—at the banks, at the homes of the bankers, and at the District Attorney's office.

When the aggrieved depositors finally arrived at the Jarmolowskys—Sender was dead by this time, but his sons were rich and presumably happy in Washington Heights—the family escaped the mob by fleeing across the rooftops. No matter; one son was convicted of mismanagement when it was discovered that with liabilities of nearly two million dollars the grandiose Jarmolowsky bank had assets of less than seven hundred thousand.

13 Congregation B'nai Israel Kalwarie, 13-15 Pike Street

This now bricked-up and graffiti'd building, built in 1903 by immigrants from the village of Kalwarie on the Polish-Lithuanian border, was once the site of a near riot.

In 1911, an "uptown" rabbi, Stephen S. Wise, was giving another of his Friday evening lectures—in English!—at Clinton Hall (151 Clinton Street). His hope was to introduce and perhaps convert members of his audience to Reform Judaism. His auditors apparently listened to him without overt hostility, but when he passed a collection basket—Orthodox Jews are not permitted to carry money on the Sabbath—a number of them were angered. They stalked out.

What to do? With the assistance of a local civic leader, those who were offended called on Judah Magnes [see stop #11], who agreed to give a series of lectures on Orthodox religious themes in the Kalwarie synagogue. Magnes was American born, a "modern" man for whom Reform Judaisim was created. Magnes, however, found it lacking in spiritual richness. As a result, thousands of young men who wanted to retain their religious traditions while participating fully in American life were eager to hear and learn from him. On the first night, storming the doors, they elbowed, pushed, and shoved so eagerly that police had to be called to restrain them.

It was amid such passions as displayed at this Pike Street *shul* (Yiddish for "synagogue") that the Young Israel movement was born. Its members took the position that Orthodoxy could be combined with speaking English, shaving their beards, and doing such scandalously American things as dancing with women. They could, they affirmed, remain true to their religion while becoming real Americans. Their position met a demonstrable need. Young Israel grew, spread to other parts of the country, and is a major force within Orthodoxy to this day.

The Eldridge Street Synagogue, looking as if its architects meant to reproduce Notre Dame.

14 | The Eldridge Street Synagogue, 12-16 Eldridge Street

Built in 1886-87 by the Herter brothers, Protestant German architects, this landmarked building, with its rose window and elaborate exterior, was the pride and joy of the Russian-Polish Congregation K'hal Adath Jeshurun (Community of the People of Israel) with Anshe Lubz (People of Lubz).

In tsarist Russia, Jews would rarely have expressed themselves in this architectural fashion. There the synagogue was usually a modest building, not immediately recognizable, in the hope that it might be overlooked during pogroms or other anti-Semitic actions.

But in America, the Golden Land, a well-to-do congregation could build expansively, and the members of K'hal Adath Jeshurun—Sender Jarmulowsky among them—certainly did. Stained glass windows! They ordered the synagogue's ark, large enough to hold twenty torahs, to be crafted in Italy out of solid walnut and inlaid with mosaic.

This and the other synagogues of the Lower East Side began to decline in the 1920s as the City's mass transit system was being extended

14

cont.

into the outer boroughs. Families who had done well in the old neighborhood followed the transit lines. And because of the religious proscription against riding on the Sabbath, the members of the Lower East Side congregations simply rebuilt their synagogues in the new neighborhoods. Such buildings as they left behind were sometimes bought by other immigrant groups, as they themselves had bought and transformed the churches abandoned by the Christians who had preceded them on the Lower East Side.

Those synagogues not bought and reconsecrated or used for other than religious purposes were usually left to deteriorate. In the case of the Eldridge Street Synagogue, however, a small congregation still gathers here on Sabbaths and holy days, and a nonprofit group continues its efforts to bring the interior and exterior back to their former glory.

Although they are in sad decline, a number of the old houses of worship are worth visiting. Their very abandonment speaks to the upward mobility of the immigrants.

Congregation Poel Zedek Anshe Ileya (Workers for Justice, People of Ileya), 128-130 Forsyth Street: The synagogue now houses the Seventh-Day Adventist Church of Union Square. Erected in 1895, the building, situated on a corner, is surely unique: its Delancey Street side has storefronts built in. The idea was to use the commercial rents to finance maintenance.

First Romanian-American Synagogue, Shaari Shomoyin (Gates of Heaven), 89 Rivington Street: The building was originally a Methodist church. The congregation acquired it in 1885, when its members outgrew their first synagogue at 70 Hester Street and began to think of themselves as *Americans* from Romania. Despite its shabby exterior, the interior is splendid and appropriately large: it seats sixteen hundred people. The Methodist parish house next door, which the Romanians turned into a talmud torah (a house of study), has been converted into apartments.

Congregation Beth Hakenesseth Mogen Avraham (Shield of Abraham), 87 Attorney Street: Built for a white Methodist congregation in 1845, it later became the Emanuel African Methodist Church and then the Erste Galitzianer Chevra (First Galician Congregation), which group adopted the current name. Just to the north of this Greek Revival building stands the old Emanuel parish house, which came to be used as a talmud torah and headquarters of a *landsmanshaft*.

15 First Cemetery of the Spanish and Portuguese Synagogue, Shearith Israel, 55-57 St. James Place

In use between 1682 and 1831, this graveyard is the oldest Jewish cemetery in the country and, with the Negro Burial Ground [see African stop #9] and the churchyard of St. Paul's Chapel (Broadway and Fulton Street), it is among the oldest in the City. It is certainly the one spot in the City that has title to the longest continuous land use.

It is open to the public only on Memorial Day, when the congregation of Shearith Israel (Remnants of Israel) commemorates Jewish participants in the American Revolution and Gershom Mendes Seixas in particular. Seixas, the synagogue's cantor, so distinguished that he served on the board of trustees of Columbia College for over thirty years, was the sole representative of the Jewish community at George Washington's inauguration.

A portion of the congregation's second cemetery, still visible on 11th Street between Fifth and Sixth avenues, was opened in 1805. Its third cemetery, dating from 1829, is located on West 21st Street between Sixth and Seventh avenues, and a small section is also viewable.

After 1852, burials were no longer permitted on Manhattan Island, although a long-standing rumor has it that a vast cemetery in Washington

Heights (spreading eastward from Riverside Drive between 153rd and 155th Streets) is the exception that proves the rule. Belonging to Wall Street's famous Trinity Church, the cemetery contains the grave of Clement Moore, author of "The Night before Christmas."

The El on Allen Street rattled windows along its entire length, but generations of New Yorkers who experienced the ride will attest that subways can never provide such pleasures. On the El, riders not pinned to the center of the cars could sightsee into lives being lived in apartments along the route.

16 | 123 Allen Street

Today a wide boulevard embracing a strip of park, Allen Street, originally fifty feet from curb to curb, was shadowed until 1942 by the Second Avenue El. Beneath it and its rattling cars in the early years of the century were illegal pool halls, gambling houses, and the Lower East Side's red-light district.

Red lights in windows were not, however, the signal of availability; handkerchiefs were. "Handkerchief girls" would cruise the street, handkerchief in hand. When a man caught a girl's eye, she would drop the handkerchief. He, in turn, would pick it up and return it; then she would lead the way to her room or to a convenient alley or rooftop.

Allen Street also catered to Chinese patrons in at least one rather well-appointed dope den. In 1913, the meticulous investigator for the *kehillah* [see stop #11] reported:

> *At 123 Allen Street, 3 flights up in the rear, left hand side going up, room 11, is a hop [narcotics] joint, owned by Abe Greenberg, who formerly owned one on 25th Street between 7th and 8th Avenues. This place is composed of two rooms, a kitchen and a bedroom. In the kitchen are two beds. In the bedroom there is a bunk upon which about 6 smokers can lay. It is made of wood, nailed to the wall and covering half of the room, and the entire length of it.*
>
> *The place is neatly furnished and the walls contain college flags. As gas fixtures there is a red and green light made so by the color of the globes. On the walls are also small signs with such sayings as "Welcome Home," "Home Sweet Home," and "Call Again."*

When the El was torn down, the City also demolished an entire row of tenements along the east side of Allen Street. As a consequence, the buildings to be seen on that side of the street are actually the backs of Orchard Street tenements. (Urban archaeologists working for The Tenement Museum at 97 Orchard Street are exploring the backyard of the Museum's site. In time, anyone walking down Allen Street should be able to see a re-creation of the privies that stood in the rear of the tenements prior to the long-contested 1903 law requiring water closets —one for every two families.)

159

To appreciate this sterile picture of the Allen Street baths, one must imagine it filled with people chattering as they entered the stalls, then more silent and contemplative as they left, warmed, clean, and rosy.

17 | Public Bath House, 133 Allen Street

Bath houses were not invented for tenement dwellers; they were first established in the City during colonial times. But as more and more City residents came to enjoy indoor plumbing, those who had to resort to bath houses were mostly poor people. And by the middle of the nineteenth century, the City was crammed with the poor—poor in pocket and poorer still in bathing facilities.

The first public bath house in the City opened in 1849 on Mott Street. In addition to bathtubs, it contained a swimming pool, a remarkable addition given that the facility was open only during the summer, when the waters of the East and North (Hudson) rivers were warm enough for a dip. Also odd is the fact that the bath, originated by the Association for Improving the Condition of the Poor, was too expensive for most of those for whom it had been built. It was not long before its putative customers went back to taking sponge baths at the washtub in the kitchen, a tub into which only small children or the household laundry could fit.

Although some charities later took up the cause of bath houses for the people, and even built some, it was not until 1895 that the state legislature stepped in to require the building of free public baths in municipalities with populations of at least fifty thousand. All by itself the Lower East Side had that many people, and the first City-built public bath, on Rivington Street, was opened, summer and winter, in 1901.

Divided by sex, the patrons received a clean towel, a bit of soap, and twenty minutes under a hot shower for two to five cents. An older generation—both of Jews and Italians—remembers them with gratitude and pleasure. This one on Allen Street remained in operation until the 1970s

EPILOGUE

Although few Jews now reside on the Lower East Side, many of the shops are shuttered on Friday evenings and on Saturdays—the Sabbath Like Italians, they own businesses but no longer live—no longer have to live—above or near the store. Like the other ethnic groups who hoped to find gold in these narrow streets, the Jews too have become part of the mainstream of America. Where do they live now? Most of them still in cities, from the upper West and East Sides of Manhattan to Miami Beach, Beverly Hills, and Tel Aviv, but also in locations far beyond the imaginings of their immigrant forebears: Research Triangle in North Carolina, Silicon Valley in California, Los Alamos in New Mexico—"Only in America."

Italian Heritage

In 1790, the year of the first federal census, only twenty families with Italian surnames were recorded as living in Manhattan. This tiny number was hardly increased in the decades that followed, and the only name to stand out among them is that of Lorenzo da Ponte. Da Ponte will be remembered (by those who remember such things) for as long as Mozart's operas are revered. Before he ever thought to accept a position in the New World as professor of Italian at Columbia University, da Ponte had written the libretti for *The Marriage of Figaro, Don Giovanni,* and *Così fan Tutte.*

During da Ponte's time in New York (from 1805 to his death in 1838), only a few hundred of his countrymen arrived in the United States each year, and those who remained in the City left few traces. Most went about their business —as musicians, cabinet makers, seamstresses —with little notice. By midcentury, when Giuseppe Garibaldi, the great patriot and soldier, took political refuge for a year on Staten Island, the numbers were still minuscule; in the entire country, there were only about three thousand.

Da Ponte, Mozart's best librettist, was present for the New York première of *Don Giovanni* in 1826—eight years after its North American première in Philadelphia but almost forty years after its first performance in Prague.

By 1860, the City was home to about fourteen hundred people who had been born in Italy, and most of them had come from the northern regions. Their occupations were diverse, ranging from well-educated professors and opera divas (Adelina Patti was the most renowned) to unschooled and unskilled dockworkers. Those at the bottom of the economic ladder included ragpickers, organ grinders, and fruit vendors who flocked to the cheapest housing available: Five Points on the Lower East Side.

Like much of the Lower East Side, Five Points, the area where Baxter and Worth streets intersect with what is now Columbus Park, was built atop badly drained marshlands, in this case directly over a freshwater pond known as the Collect. At first, given its convenient location—just a few blocks from City Hall and the centers of commerce—prosperous families resided there. All too soon, however, the land began to sink and swamplike odors to rise. Indeed, Collect Pond was described as "stagnant and mephitic" as early as 1796.

The prosperous moved elsewhere and the poor—initially German, then Irish—moved in. What had been single-family homes belonging to the well-to-do turned into cramped quarters for any number of impoverished families. Their replacement with tenements came after the worst days of Five Points.

Not too long after gangs of Irish toughs had made Five Points notorious [see Irish stop #10], Italian immigration to the United States began to pick up. From fewer than two thousand in the decade between 1841 and 1850, it rose to over nine thousand in 1851–60 and to almost fifty-six thousand in 1871–80. Then the dam broke. Italian immigration increased to over three hundred thousand in the following ten years, more than doubled in the last decade of the nineteenth century, and at its peak—between 1901 and 1914, when World War I stopped the flow—over three million Italians were recorded as having arrived in America. (Like statistics in general, these numbers are misleading. Although great masses of Italians did, of course, come to the United States, many of them repatriated themselves one or more times—and were recounted each time they returned.)

Not all immigrant Italians settled in New York; New Jersey, Pennsylvania, California, and Massachusetts also absorbed the newcomers. But the City was, as usual, a strong magnet for immigrants crossing the Atlantic. Pockets of their compatriots were already here.

What had happened to create and then spur the exodus? Until the 1860s, the states of southern Italy had forbidden emigration. After

With the trained monkey atop a barrel organ, these children were being "taught" to play in a small orchestra. Apart from a few pennies sent to their families, the contributions from passers-by would be pocketed by the *padroni* who provide them with housing and this all too common form of education.

the country was unified in 1861, those laws were revoked. And the peasants of the south, who had endured high rents and heavy taxation, exhausted, deforested lands, earthquakes, and epidemics, were at last free to escape.

Among the earliest to depart were children sent abroad to earn money as itinerant musicians. Rounded up and employed by labor brokers called *padroni*, the children played hurdy-gurdies and barrel organs on the streets of New York (London and Paris as well) and were thus able to send part of their earnings home to families as poor as themselves.

Even after the practice was made illegal in 1885, *padroni* continued to recruit adult laborers, to pay their passage to America, and, at considerable profit to themselves despite the cost of providing food and lodging, to hire out the men in work gangs to American employers.

W hen these southerners arrived, they were lumped together statistically as emigrants from the newly unified nation of Italy. They, on the contrary, identified themselves as belonging to a region: to Calabria, Apulia, Campania, Abruzzi, and Basilicata or the island of Sicily. Even more narrowly, they identified themselves with their villages. And that is how many settled in: as villagers renting, where possible even in the same tenement, on a regionally homogeneous street. Mulberry Street, for example, became distinctly Neapolitan (i.e., from Campania); Mott Street between Broome and Grand was claimed by the Calabresi; Hester Street was Apulian. The length of Elizabeth Street was not only Sicilian, it was settled town by town: from Houston south to Spring, the immigrants came from Palermo; from Spring to Grand they came from Siacca; from Grand to Hester,

In front of 56 Mulberry Street, immigrants replicate their homeland. Not only do the newcomers maintain their Old Country attire (who could afford new clothing?), but what look like stalks of wheat in the tub at the right may be lavender, the fragrant herb still sold on the sidewalks of Italian towns.

167

from Messina. (Apart from a pocket of Genoese on Baxter Street, any northern Italians who came mostly settled elsewhere in the City.)

Like earlier ethnics, the immigrant Italians were heavily male. And not all of them wished to remain in America. Like the Chinese, many intended to work for a while and then return home to their families with the money they had earned. They were able to act on this plan for two reasons: jobs for unskilled laborers were abundant (digging the subways, excavating for Grand Central Terminal), and steamships plied the Atlantic ever more cheaply and swiftly. The voyage could now take as little as ten days. No longer did a trip require two or more months of one's life spent amid stomachturning foulness.

Although steerage was never to resemble a holiday at sea, the conditions aboard passenger-carrying steamships that ferried the Italians to America (and back) were a far cry from the pestilential wretchedness endured by the Germans in the 1840s and the Irish in the 1850s. In fact, two-way transportation was so feasible that between 1907 and 1911 more people flowed east to Europe than came in the opposite direction

This back-and-forthing had the full approval of the Italian government, which viewed the movement as a problem solver. Underemployed or jobless or landless Italians sitting and talking in village squares might have become disaffected, might have caused political unrest. How much safer for the government to encourage the men to go to America, to send a portion of their wages back to wives and family, to return home with more dollars in their pockets, then to repeat the cycle. On such round trips a village economy could survive.

While obviously advantageous to Italy as a nation and to the families receiving sustenance, this bird-of-passage behavior—which also benefited the American economy by reducing the number of unemployed during periods of depression—enraged some Americans. These xenophobes looked at the Italians and decided they drank too much, fought among themselves, gambled, and consorted with prostitutes. Then, in a final insult to the City and country, they took their money back home to spend. Who needed such immigrants?

The Chinese had been excluded by law in 1882. The Italians, although never excluded, were among those from Southern and Eastern Europe whose immigration was restricted by the quotas set in 1924.

Spearheaded by Jacob Riis, Al Smith, and a police commissioner named Theodore Roosevelt, the slums of Mulberry Bend were replaced by Columbus Park in 1892.

Italian Tour

1 | Columbus Park

Now in constant use by the residents of Chinatown—at certain hours, elderly Chinese women can be observed doing tai chi exercises —this park replaced the slums of Mulberry Bend in 1892.

The Bend, named for the spot where Mulberry Street curves toward the west, was among the most squalid slums in the world and was certainly the most fearsome in the City. Already exhausted by the Germans and Irish, the housing taken over by immigrant Italians must have been unspeakable. But the area's notoriety was due to Jacob Riis, the Danish immigrant journalist and reformer, who photographed Mulberry Bend and its inhabitants for his articles in the *Tribune* and *Evening Sun*.

Collected in Riis's *How the Other Half Lives* (1890), these reports horrified even the complacent. The whole block—from Bayard south to Park, from Baxter east to Mulberry—was razed. In its place came fresh air and light, and greenery under which Italian musicians played familiar airs, men rolled bocce balls, and children gamboled. On such festive occasions as saints' days and Columbus Day, food vendors assembled and the air rang with band concerts and the crack of fireworks. But as with the widening of Allen Street and the creation of Seward Park [see Jewish stop #4], there were now fewer houses in which to live. So, ironically, population density grew.

2 Church of the Transfiguration, 25 Mott Street

Originally built for English Lutherans in 1801, this church building has been Roman Catholic since 1853. And although a small Italian population still worships there, it is now overwhelmingly Chinese, with services offered in both Mandarin and Cantonese.

In the 1890s, as a Roman Catholic church, it simultaneously served both Irish and Italians. While the Irish attended Mass in the main sanctuary, the Italians—one of whom was young Jimmy Durante, whose father had a barber shop on Mulberry Street—took communion from an Italian priest in the basement. Father McLoughlin tried to persuade the nearly twelve hundred Italian parishioners to join with his Irish flock, but they would have none of it. (One might guess that the Irish were none too happy with the idea either.) Quite naturally, the Italians much preferred a priest who knew of their lives and who could counsel and comfort in their own language. By choice, but without pleasure, they remained in the basement until 1902, when the first Italian pastor was named. Among the occasional worshippers at the now Italian Church of the Transfiguration was the world's most famous tenor, Enrico Caruso.

The role of the Catholic Church in the lives of Italian immigrants is problematic. In New York the Church was dominated by the Irish, whose more reserved and conservative approach to religion was alien to Italians. As a consequence,

171

2

proselytizers from most of the Protestant denominations set up missions in Italian neighborhoods. Nationwide by 1916, over fifty thousand formerly Roman Catholic Italians converted.

But not all Catholic churches felt alien to the new immigrants. The now-demolished St. Joachim's at 26 Roosevelt Street was particularly welcoming, and by 1905 its membership was entirely Italian. Along with a kindergarten that enrolled two hundred children, it celebrated five Masses each Sunday to accommodate its membership of some twenty thousand parishioners, many of whom were ragpickers. They scavenged clothing, metal, wood, and whatever other odds and ends they could find on the streets and brought the refuse to the church basement, where they sorted and bundled it and then sold it to junkmen.

Italian laborers in front of City Hall constructing Manhattan's first subway.

3 ## Public School #23, 70 Mulberry Street

This school, along with one at 62 Mott Street (now the New York Chinese School) and another at a now-demolished building at 222 Mott Street, enrolled many Italian children. Enrolled them and often lost them. Schooling was rarely popular with children of immigrants; and parents whose folk philosophy included the adage "Never educate your children beyond yourself" remembered and rejected the schooling they themselves had received. (The schools of southern Italy were poorly financed, badly maintained, and employed teachers who were poorly prepared.)

Many Italian parents preferred to send their children to work. There they would be disciplined; there they would earn money to contribute to the family income; there they would not be subject to the most objectionable effects of instruction: questioning their parents and disrespecting their elders—simply not acceptable in a culture in which fathers emphatically knew best.

Given active discouragement from many Italian families—and families were all-important—children did poorly in school, found themselves falling behind their non-Italian classmates, getting left back, and finally dropping out in embarrassed relief.

The pattern—and it was not uncommon even among immigrant and first-generation Eastern European Jews, whose eagerness for education has been much exaggerated—lasted well into the twentieth century. Italians had the highest school dropout rate of any immigrant group in the City. As a consequence, until the pattern changed in the 1970s with open admission to the City's colleges, Italian men were more highly represented among laborers than any other white ethnic group in America apart from Hispanics.

The pattern might have been correctible had Italians founded more than a few of their own parochial schools, but the parochial system had already been established by the Irish. And although Italian orders of priests and nuns taught at some of those schools, few other Italians or Italian-Americans were qualified or inclined to be teachers. Additionally, many Italians in America continued to view themselves as birds of passage, as temporary residents, and many retained a low regard for formal education.

3 Nevertheless, even a few years of schooling meant that Italian children learned English and became indispensable to their parents for communicating with landlords, lawyers, and the petty officialdom of the City. So despite all, they became the very opposite of the silent and obedient children common in the Old World.

Proud Italians parading with the statue of San Rocco during the saint's festival around 1915. Also known as St. Roch, the saint is invoked in all countries against contagious diseases. Legend has it that, suffering from plague and hunger, Rocco/Roch was befriended by a dog who fed him each day with a piece of bread stolen from its master's table.

4 ## Church of the Most Precious Blood, 113 Baxter Street

San Donato, San Rocco, San Gennaro, Santa Rosalia, Sant'Agata, San Giuseppe—these were among the patron saints of the southern Italians on the Lower East Side.

In their honor, processions, blocks in length, moved through the streets from one church to another amid the noise of firecrackers. Hundreds of candles burned to light the streets while musicians, seated on improvised stands built over the sidewalks, played opera tunes and march music. (Gian-Carlo Menotti's opera *The Saint of Bleecker Street* is set at one such event.)

From the Church of the Most Precious Blood, built in 1892, the great festival in honor of San Gennaro began every September. Even today his statue is visible in the window of a men's club down the street, and the festival still continues, with thousands of people now of all races and religions participating in what has become one of the most joyous of the City's street fairs. Few or none of the revelers know they join in celebration of Janarius, patron saint of Naples, who is credited with delivering Neapolitans from the plague of 1497 and the fearsome eruptions of Mt. Vesuvius.

The starting point for the festival of San Rocco was 273 Mott Street. Acting on their belief in his power to cure illness, each August 16 immigrants from Basilicata (the region about which Carlo Levi wrote in his heart-rending *Christ Stopped at Eboli*) would bring out St. Rocco's shrine and attach to it an assortment of wax body parts for which they were asking cures. Those who had no particular need for a cure showed their gratitude by pinning dollar bills to the shrine.

Festivals—*feste*—although also held for secular figures like Garibaldi and Columbus, were primarily associated with saints. Religious *feste* also served as name-day parties for those carrying the name of the saint being celebrated. And special pastries—like the fried dumpling eaten with sugar or honey, the *zeppole* of San Giuseppe —served as a kind of birthday cake for the name-carrying celebrants of the community. Saints whose names proliferated were the subjects of such large festivities that the parties went on for days.

The sign pointing to Banca Stabile at the corner promises superlative service. Patrons can also wire money orders to their families abroad.

5 | Stabile Bank, Southwest Corner of Mulberry and Grand Streets

Like earlier immigrants, the Italians preferred to do their banking with people who spoke their dialect. The Stabile Bank, in offices that now house a real estate concern, was one of the many small "regional" banks that sprang up in Little Italy. Even today one can see its tile floor, pressed tin ceiling, iron tellers' cages, and, back in a rear corner, the old vault.

In addition to regular banking services, which included the transmission of millions of dollars each year sent home to Italy, these regional banks sold steamship tickets and offered translation services, needed when patrons confronted English-language legal documents, postal orders, and the like.

Another of the Mulberry Street banks (cum travel agencies) was one run by Don Angelo Legniti, an honored member of the Italian colony and key member of the *Società Filo-drammatica Italiana* (founded in 1878), which by 1902 was located at the address of still another bank, at 80 1/2 Mulberry.

The *Società*'s presentations were staged wherever there was space, one year at 44-46 Houston Street, another year at the Hotel Roma at 152-154 East 42nd Street. It offered Italian classics as well as presentations with a distinctly New York flavor: one, a drama in six acts, was called *I Misteri di*

Mulberry. It also commemorated patriotic events, such as Garibaldi's entrance into Naples.

Audiences got their money's worth. Between the acts, acrobats or dancers or the orchestra would perform, and a *gran ballo*, a grand community ball, would always conclude the evening. Only the musicians were regularly paid. The actors typically worked out of love.

However lacking in refinement, performances were enthusiastically received. According to one observer:

> *On Thursday nights there were practically three performances going on....The players themselves gave one with a wary eye on the prompter's box. The prompter gave another—complete, strong-voiced, and about two seconds ahead of the official rendition. And the audience managed to give a third—laughing, applauding, shushing noisy children, and hissing in a body.* (As quoted in Maxine Seller [ed.], *Ethnic Theater in the United States*)

We can imagine with what additional relish the audience responded to plays about neighborhood events. After a local woman was convicted of murdering her husband, the *Società* staged *Chiara, la Condannata a Morte* (Clara, the One Condemned to Death).

Such events were sometimes the occasion for benefits for specific charities, the Italian Hospital, or various schools. The *Società* also contributed to Gaetano Russo's 1892 statue of Christopher Columbus at Columbus Circle, and in 1887 it gave a benefit for the victims of cholera in Messina. Amount raised, $59.60 after expenses.

Fund-raising from unskilled laborers, for whom "benefit performance" was an alien concept, could not have been easy, but the difficulty in no way diminished their generosity. The immigrants gave away huge sums—seven hundred fifty million dollars is the figure often cited—but by culture and tradition, they gave it as family members abroad to families at home in villages.

E. Rossi and Co., 191 Grand Street

The original store was opened in 1902 at #187 by immigrants from Naples to sell Italian-language books, phonograph records, sheet music (printed in America), and wooden music rolls. When the market for music rolls died—radio and movies increasingly replaced participatory entertainment among all groups—the Rossis sold the first location and reopened here, still selling books and records to an Italian clientele most comfortable buying opera recordings by Caruso and Galli-Curci and Rosa Ponselle (the legendary American-born soprano) from shopkeepers who spoke their language. Migliaccio [see stop #7] was a frequent visitor.

For a sense of how the neighborhood's needs have changed, Rossi's, its old books and classical records no longer for sale, today stocks souveniers and some popular recordings by Italians like Connie Frances and Mario Lanza. A student of immigration notes that when tee shirts and buttons read "Kiss Me, I'm Italian," the neighborhood caters largely to tourists.

Migliaccio in one of his comic Neapolitan immigrant guises.

7 Caffè Roma, 385 Broome Street

Caffè Roma, which still serves authentic Italian coffee and desserts, was known in the early 1900s as Caffè Ronca. In the 1920s, it was a favorite gathering spot for Italian actors. They were drawn to Ronca's because the wildly popular Eduard Migliaccio took his morning coffee there. Migliaccio, who specialized in comedy, created the much-loved character of Farfariello, a stereotypical Neapolitan immigrant who spoke both English and Italian atrociously. The funny, broad-stroke portrayal was not viewed as insensitive or insulting. By evoking laughter, it transmuted individual pain into community pleasure.

Still another *caffè*—the Villa Vittorio Emanuele, on Mulberry Street near Canal—housed the oldest Italian theater in the City. The *caffè* charged no admission; it made its money on the drinks consumed, and—until they rebelled—the actors made theirs from contributions they solicited from whatever patrons happened to remain at the end of the evening.

No reliable list exists of how many of these coffee houses there were or for how long they operated. But the regional identification of each was strong, and people who had per-

7

cont.

formed in Italy—or who had wanted to—found appropriate audiences. Performances went beyond simple acting and singing to include mime, comedy acts, and portable puppet shows. And because few professional performers emigrated to the United States, sometimes neighborhood barbers and street vendors also got a chance to take the stage.

8

Old Saint Patrick's Cathedral, 260-264 Mulberry Street

In 1882, an Italian subcongregation was formed here in what was another Irish-dominated Catholic church—a subcongregation that met and worshipped in the basement. Two Italian priests handled baptisms, marriages, and sick calls and said the Masses. Only children attending the parochial and Sunday schools mixed with the Irish upstairs.

Italians were not barred from the main chancel, any more than they were at the Church of the Transfiguration [stop #2]; they simply, and understandably, declined to attend. It cost five cents at the door to get a seat at Mass. Paying hurt their purses; standing, when others did not, wounded their pride.

Even though they lacked sympathy for the American separation of church and state, the Irish congregants thought it natural to pay for the upkeep of church and clergy. Their experience included being subject to English rule. Until the late 1870s, this entailed their being made to support the (Anglican) Church of Ireland. Italians, on the other hand, were accustomed to an established church, whose activities were state supported. Why should they be required to pay for the spiritual equivalent of air and sunshine?

Religiously, too, there were conflicts. From the Italian point of view, an Irish-dominated Catholic Church placed more stress on obedience than on joy. From the Irish point of view,

the Italians, who held boisterous outdoor celebrations in extravagant worship of their saints,
were little more than pagan idolators.

The basement congregation was eventually dis-
solved. However comforting the division along
ethnic lines, it underlined the worshippers' identification with their homelands; and by implying
strong allegiance to a foreign land and an alien
religion, it gave support to nativist resentments.

Within Old St. Pat's, visitors can see evidence of
the congregational transition. On the wall where
the pastors are commemorated, the names eventually change from Irish to Italian. Soon, no
doubt, the ethnic identification of the names will
change again to meet needs of a congregation
that is increasingly Dominican.

9 Fourteenth Ward Industrial School, Mulberry Street Opposite Old St. Patrick's Cathedral

This co-op residence was originally a school
built in 1889 by the Children's Aid Society (its
initials are visible in the upper pediment) with
funds from John Jacob Astor III.

The school represented both Protestant philanthropy and fear. Well-to-do New Yorkers like
Astor genuinely wanted immigrant children to
be able to quit the slums. To enable them to do
so, the children needed skills that an industrial
school could teach.

But they also wanted to turn Italian-speaking
ragamuffins into proper New Yorkers, capable of
becoming self-disciplined employees, ideally of
the Protestant faith. So along with skills, the children were to learn English and to adopt middle-
class American standards of cleanliness, table
manners, and attitudes toward law and order.

In the hope of converting the Italians to "civilization," the Episcopal diocese even built a church in the neighborhood—the Church of San Salvatore (359 Broome at Elizabeth Street)—and staffed it with Italian-speaking ministers. It is likely that to stop defections, the Catholic archdiocese built Most Holy Crucifix across the street at 378 Broome Street and staffed it with Italian priests.

Following the pattern, now that the neighborhood is home to relatively few Italians, San Salvatore has been transformed into the Holy Trinity Ukrainian Orthodox Church. But above the doorway, the faint outlines of "Church of San Salvatore" remain visible.

Being a garment worker did not necessarily mean toiling in a factory. A sweatshop could be one's own kitchen. These women were expected to tend the children and sew at the same time. And to increase their productivity, stitches could always be added while waiting for the water to boil.

10 Elizabeth Street

From Houston to Canal, Elizabeth Street was favored by Sicilians, and like all of Little Italy— like poor immigrant neighborhoods everywhere and always—it was fertile ground for crime. Both perpetrators and victims, and often the policemen trying to clean things up, were Italian. Indeed, the City's first bomb squad, whose later fame included the investigation of the massive detonation at the World Trade Center in 1993, was headed by and composed of Italian members of the Police Department.

The Sicilian-born Mafia was (and is) a highly structured criminal organization; its Neapolitian version, the Camorra, was no less structured. The unorganized Black Hand—it was not regional—carried out an American version of an extortion racket that had thrived in some parts of Italy for generations.

The Black Hand was responsible for a bombing at 147 Elizabeth Street in 1913. Some of its members had been successfully demanding money from merchants and well-off families on the block. Pay and we let you alone. One fruit vendor refused to fork over. The bomb that exploded in front of his shop blew the windows out of eight tenements (from #145 to #152), a German Lutheran church, and its parsonage.

Beginning in the early 1890s, Elizabeth Street between Broome and Spring became the site of clothing factories in which many single Italian women were employed as sewing machine operators. (Married women did not go out to work. They labored at home, "finishing" garments: they cuffed pants, worked buttonholes, and stitched lapels for rates that varied greatly, but most women could earn about two dollars a week, especially if their children helped.)

To start with, some Italian men were also employed in the factories—as pressers or, like their female relatives, as operators—but soon they began to work at such skilled jobs as cutting and designing. By 1905 Italians had become major players in the garment industry.

At least to midcentury, barbers were customarily Italian. Outside, a red and white striped barber pole reflected the fact that barbers once also served as surgeons and dentists.

11 | 233-235 Elizabeth Street

Donna Gabaccia, an historian who has studied this tenement building, one of many in the neighborhood, reports that in 1905 it housed a total of twenty-seven families: one hundred nine people in twenty apartments. Only nine of the families had been in America for more than five years, and about half of the residents had relatives in the same building. Their occupations are not without interest: twenty-one laborers, twelve finishers, nine garment workers, three fruit peddlers, two masons, two barbers, and—one each—gilder, iron worker, bricklayer, laundress, hod carrier, and artificial-flower maker. Fifty-five employed people—of whom as many as twenty-three could have been female—among twenty-seven families.

Eventually, Italians were to be as prominent in fruit and vegetable stores as Koreans are today. They would also be overrepresented as barbers, waiters, longshoremen, and as deliverers of coal and ice. But among them were also brilliantly skilled artisans, men who left their mark on the City in the form of ornate stone facades that grace Ellis Island and the mansions that spot locations like Riverside Drive.

12 | St. Anthony of Padua's Roman Catholic Church, 155 Sullivan Street

Begun in the 1860s, prior to the mass migration, and not completed until 1888, this church was dedicated to the wonder-working saint who is said to have spoken so splendidly in every language that even the fish listened with pleasure. Sited in a more prosperous part of the area, where Italian families often moved when they had done well on the Lower East Side, the parish of St. Anthony was, according to *Harper's Monthly,* "attended by a superior class of Italians, all apparently prosperous and at peace with their environment"—in a word, by "northerners."

The distinction *Harper's* made between northern and southern Italians was obviously an invidious one. Its roots lay in the fact that very few skilled workers and still fewer professionals chose to emigrate. The mass of immigrants were poorly educated peasants, primarily from the agricultural regions of the south.

Peasants are "different"—different certainly from the non-peasants who get their opinions into print. No peasant, for instance, no matter what his origins, speaks the formal language of his country—in this case the Tuscan dialect brought to literary perfection by Dante and Petrarch. As Ignazio Silone, a southerner of a later generation, wrote in the foreword to his novel *Fontamara* (1930):

> *Do not imagine for one moment that the inhabitants of Fontamara [Abruzzi] talk Italian. For us Italian is a language learnt at school, like Latin, French or Esperanto. Italian is like a foreign language, a dead language, a language the vocabulary and grammar of which developed without any connection with us or our mode of thinking or expressing ourselves.*

But dialect marks people and snobbery will out, even though pure Italian is still not widely spoken by Italian nationals, especially if educated before World War II.

Like the educated and urban German Jews encountering Eastern European coreligionists for the first time in New York, educated Italians were embarrassed to be associated with their peasant compatriots. The German Jews set up organizations to "improve" their brethren: immigrant aid societies, clinics, classes to prepare for citizenship, foundations to foster the social and educational needs of youngsters. As a rule, educated Italians did not. And they had good reason not to if we consider the number of Italians who repatriated themselves. According to Thomas Kessner, who has studied immigrant mobility in the City, in just the four years 1907–11 "the rate of annual return had spiraled to 150,000 individuals, averaging 73 repatriates for every 100 Italian immigrants." There was thought to be no point in building institutions for people who were not going to be around to use them.

But some evidence of ethnic pride should be made manifest. Thus, the Italian community erected statues to their great men—in Manhattan, to Garibaldi in Washington Square Park [see stop #14], to Columbus (59th Street and Columbus Circle), and to the immortal composer Giuseppe Verdi (73rd Street and Amsterdam Avenue). The statues had value beyond the inspirational: they helped to create a sense of commonality among immigrants who otherwise identified only with people from their own villages and regions.

A two-bank headline and a full front page were only the beginning of the reportage of the fire at the Triangle Shirtwaist factory. Despite public outrage over the deaths, those responsible got away scot free.

13 Triangle Shirtwaist Factory, 19 Washington Place

On Saturday afternoon, March 25, 1911, a fire broke out on the eighth, ninth, and tenth floors of this building, now owned by New York University. Workers, mostly women, found themselves unable to escape down the stairs because the managers, citing theft and loss of work time, had locked the doors. Once they arrived, firemen could not reach the upper floors with their ladders. Some of the women jumped to their deaths on the sidewalk; others fell from the fire escape that twisted under them; still others were crushed against doors that opened inward.

Death toll: one hundred forty-six people, almost all of them unmarried women. Of them, one-third were Italian, generally between the ages of sixteen and twenty-five.

Until this appalling fire, Italian workers had generally taken little interest in labor unions. Because of their peasant background, they came to America with no experience of trade unionism. In fact, many of them had been convinced to scab in the general strike against the shirtwaist owners in 1909 [see Jewish stop #2]. To some degree, this event helped turn them around.

Soon some all-Italian locals were formed in the garment workers' union. Soon workplace-safety legislation was passed in Albany. But immigrant women are still at risk. Today's sweatshops (there are some on Mott Street) may be quite as perilous for their workers as was the building which once housed the Triangle factory.

The statue of Garibaldi in Washington Square Park was a favorite place for Italians to socialize and talk politics—local, national, and international. Did the photographer scare them off?

14   Statue of Garibaldi, Washington Square Park

One of the great heroes of Italy, Giuseppe Garibaldi (1807-82) was born in France and lived for a time in South America, where he fought in the Uruguayan civil war. But his fame rests in military achievements leading to the unification of Italy. In 1860, with a volunteer army—the Red Shirts—he conquered, and then turned over to the king of Sardinia, the kingdom of the Two Sicilies (Sicily and Naples). The next year, what we know today as Italy—but still minus Venetia and Rome—became united under the Sardinian king, Victor Emmanuel II. (Venetia was absorbed in 1866, Rome in 1870.)

The statue, a gathering spot for Italians who lived nearby, was also something of an embarrassment to them. According to Camillo Cianfarra in his *Diary of an Emigrant* (1904), this 1888 statue, presented to the City by the Italians of New York, shows Garibaldi, left foot extended, drawing his sword with his right hand. Such a motion, if completed, would cause him to slice into his left knee. The sculptor, Giovanni Turini, was told of the mistake, but he died before he could correct it.

15 Greenwich House, 26-28 Jones Street

Now private residences, these houses were the original site of the Cooperative Social Settlement Society (Greenwich House), founded in 1902. The settlement moved to its present location at 29 Barrow Street in 1917.

Mary Simkhovitch, the founder, never became as famous as her contemporaries, Lillian Wald of the Henry Street Settlement [see Jewish stop #8] or Jane Addams of Chicago's Hull House, but her work was no less valuable. She chose to put her settlement house in this neighborhood because of its large and largely unserved Italian population. Or perhaps "underserved" would be more accurate, given the size and needs of the population.

Also ministering to Italians was Mother Frances Xavier Cabrini, who would become the first (naturalized) American saint. In 1889, with a half dozen sisters from the missionary order she had founded in Italy, she established one of the few Italian parochial schools in Brooklyn, an orphanage in Manhattan, and, in a tenement on

Pictured in 1910, Mother Cabrini (center, facing away) and a group of Missionary Sisters of the Sacred Heart. With only six of the sisters and a few dollars in hand, she had been sent to minister to the Italians who were arriving in the City by the thousands every month.

FRANK LESLIE'S
ILLUSTRATED
WEEKLY
NEW YORK, MARCH 11, 1894.

Although these social workers are visiting a Jewish-manned sweatshop, their haughty looks would have been the same, and would have been responded to in the same way—fear!—when they inspected an Italian sweatshop.

East 12th Street, a small hospital named for Columbus. (Today, renamed and merged with the Italian Hospital, the Cabrini Medical Center is a significant complex on East 19th Street. Mother Cabrini herself is entombed in the chapel of Cabrini High School in Washington Heights.)

The Italian Benevolent Association at 215 Spring Street also worked for the greater good by helping to put the exploiting *padroni* out of business. (These labor contractors flourished even after they were made illegal.) The Association, which was founded in 1889, referred Italian immigrants directly to employers requiring factory workers, miners, layers of railroad track, and so on, and made it clear to government officials and labor leaders that the men had not been imported for the purpose; they came of their own free will.

There was also a Society for the Protection of Italian Immigrants. From its offices at 17 Pearl Street, it offered advice on jobs, housing, and transportation to other cities, and for one year (1903) it ran a branch office at 159 Mulberry Street. Such service organizations were supported in part by local Italians who had already made their way in the City and in part by the Italian government, which had its own reasons for wanting its emigrants to thrive.

But Greenwich House had a different emphasis. Mrs. Simkhovitch's settlement provided a baby clinic, classes in English and carpentry, and many social activities. And she herself, well aware of where power lay, fought for the passage of protective labor laws and urged Italian factory workers, especially women, to join labor unions.

The Italian community was not always welcoming. Most settlement workers were what today we would call WASPs (Mrs. Simkhovitch was born Mary Kingsbury in Chestnut Hill, Massachusetts). And although they were infinitely well meaning, ultimate success involved imposing some of their own ideas on their clients. For instance, Mrs. Simkhovitch had trouble convincing mothers to let their children attend fresh-air camps in the summer or to feed them breakfast cereal. Cereal seems to have been something of an *idée fixe:*

> *Once at the [charity] school, I remember the teacher gave each child a bag of oatmeal to take home. This food was supposed to make you big and strong....My father examined the stuff, tested it with his fingers. To him, it was the kind of bran that we gave to pigs in Avigliano. "What kind of a school is this?" he shouted. "They give us the food of animals to eat and send it home to us with our children."* (Leonard Covello, *The Heart Is the Teacher* as quoted in Ewen's *Immigrant Women in the Land of Dollars*).

Not unexpectedly, the settlement workers sometimes appeared intrusive and bossy when they were trying to help. In 1907, for example, Greenwich House workers attempted to visit every family in Little Italy to warn of the dangers of diphtheria. They also visited homes to investigate the conditions under which women were employed at garment finishing and artificial-flower making. One can imagine what hard-working Italian immigrant women made of these intrusions.

EPILOGUE

Although their shops remain, few Italians now reside in Little Italy. They live on Staten Island or in the northern reaches of the Bronx, on Long Island, or anywhere else New Yorkers have chosen to settle once they've left Manhattan. They are now so much a part of mainstream America that the first woman to run for vice-president on a national ticket was Italian, and an Italian man, governor of New York for twelve years, disappointed millions of Democrats when he turned down the opportunity to run for president in 1992. (A similar disappointment was felt by millions of Republicans when an African-American turned down the same opportunity in 1996.) In sum, the descendants of New York's Italian immigrants represent another success story arising from the Lower East Side.

Bibliography

General

American Social History Project. *Who Built America?* 2 vols. New York: Pantheon Books, 1989.

Ernst, Robert. *Immigrant Life in New York City, 1825–1863.* Empire State Historical Publication XXXVII. Port Washington, NY: Ira J. Friedman, Inc., 1965.

Federal Writers' Project. *New York City Guide.* New York: Random House, 1939.

Gold, Joyce. *From Windmills to the World Trade Center.* New York: Old Warren Road Press, 1982.

Goldstone, Harmon, and Martha Dalrymple. *History Preserved: A Guide to New York City Landmarks and Historic Districts.* New York: Schocken Books, 1976.

Grafton, James. *New York in the 19th Century.* New York: Dover, 1980.

Jackson, Kenneth T. (ed.). *The Encyclopedia of New York City.* New Haven: Yale University Press and New York: The New-York Historical Society, 1995.

James, Henry. *Washington Square.* New York: New American Library, 1979.

Jones, Maldwyn Allen. *American Immigration,* 2nd edition. Chicago and London: University of Chicago Press, 1992.

Lockwood, Charles. *Manhattan Moves Uptown.* Boston: Houghton Mifflin Co., 1976.

Miller, Kenneth D., and Ethel Prince Miller. *The People Are the City.* New York: The Macmillan Co., 1962.

Roosevelt, Theodore. *An Autobiography.* New York: The Macmillan Co., 1919.

Stansell, Christine. *City of Women: Sex and Class in New York, 1789–1860.* Urbana: University of Illinois Press, 1967.

Takaki, Ronald. *A Different Mirror: A History of Multicultural America.* Boston: Little, Brown and Co., 1993.

Thernstrom, Stephen (ed.). *Harvard Encyclopedia of American Ethnic Groups.* Cambridge: Harvard University Press, 1980.

Willensky, Elliot, and Norval White. *AIA Guide to New York City,* 3rd edition. New York: Harcourt Brace Jovanovich, 1988.

African/Black

Diehl, Lorraine B. "Skeletons in the Closet: Uncovering the Rich History of the Slaves of New York," *New York,* October 5, 1992.

Grossi, Elizabeth L. " 'It Is Worth That Makes the Man': The First Generation of African-American Leaders in New York City." Unpublished master's thesis, Hunter College, 1993.

Limmer, Ruth. "Tom Hunter, Novelist," *The Hunter Magazine,* Winter 1988.

New York Times, Week in Review, February 28, 1993, p. 5. "Canonizing a Black: Saint or Uncle Tom?" February 23, 1992.

Washington, Margaret (ed.). *Narrative of Sojourner Truth.* New York: Vintage Classics, 1993.

Chinese

Barth, Gunther. *Bitter Strength: A History of the Chinese in the United States, 1850–1870.* Cambridge: Harvard University Press, 1964.

Spence, Jonathan. *The Search for Modern China.* New York: W. W. Norton & Co., 1990.

Takaki, Ronald. *A Different Mirror: A History of Multicultural America.* Boston: Little, Brown and Co., 1993.

Tung, William L. *The Chinese in America, 1820–1973*. Ethnic Chronology Series No. 14. Dobbs Ferry, NY: Oceana Publications, Inc., 1974.

Eastern European Jews

Baker, Ray Stannard. *American Chronicle*. New York: Scribner's. 1945.

Dawidowicz, Lucy S. *On Equal Terms: Jews in America 1881–1981*. New York: Holt, Rinehart and Winston, 1982.

Epstein, Melech. *Jewish Labor in U.S.A., 1882–1914*. New York: Ktav Publishing House, Inc., 1969.

Ewen, Elizabeth. *Immigrant Women in the Land of Dollars: Life and Culture on the Lower East Side, 1890–1925*. New York: Monthly Review Press, 1985.

Feingold, Henry (ed.). *The Jewish People in America*, 5 vols. Baltimore: American Jewish Historical Society and Johns Hopkins University Press, 1992.

Fischel, Jack, and Sanford Pinsker (eds.). *Jewish American History and Culture: An Encyclopedia*. New York: Garland Publishing Co., 1992.

Glenn, Susan. *Daughters of the Shtetl: Life and Labor in the Immigrant Generation*. Ithaca: Cornell University Press, 1990.

Howe, Irving. *World of Our Fathers*. New York: Harcourt Brace Jovanovich, 1976.

Karp, Abraham (ed.). *Golden Door to America*. New York: Viking Press, 1976.

Moore, Deborah Dash (ed.). *Eastern European Jews in Two Worlds: Studies from the YIVO Annual*. Evanston: North-western University Press and the YIVO Institute for Jewish Research, 1990.

Riis, Jacob. *The Battle with the Slums*. New York: Garrett Press, 1970.

Rischin, Moses. *The Promised City: New York's Jews, 1870–1914*. Cambridge: Harvard University Press, 1962.

Sachar, Howard. *A History of the Jews in America*. New York: Alfred A. Knopf, 1992.

Sanders, Ronald. *The Downtown Jews*. New York: Harper & Row, 1969.

Spewack, Bella. *Streets: A Memoir of the Lower East Side*. New York: The Feminist Press, 1995.

German

Ernst, Robert. *Immigrant Life in New York City 1825–1860*. New York: Kings Crown Press, 1949.

Gompers, Samuel. *Seventy Years of Life and Labor*. Edited and introduced by Nick Salvatore. New York: ILR Press, 1984.

Nadel, Stanley. *Little Germany: Ethnicity, Religion, and Class in New York City, 1845–80*. Urbana: University of Illinois Press, 1990.

Irish

Asbury, Herbert. *The Gangs of New York*. New York: Alfred A. Knopf, 1928.

Blessing, Patrick J. "The Irish," in *Harvard Encyclopedia of American Ethnic Groups*, Stephen Thernstrom, ed. Cambridge: Harvard University Press, 1980.

Dolan, Jay P. *The Immigrant Church: New York's Irish and German Catholics, 1815–1865*. Notre Dame, IN: University of Notre Dame Press, 1975/1983.

Glazer, Nathan, and Daniel P. Moynihan. *Beyond the Melting Pot*. Cambridge: MIT Press, 1970.

McCadden, Joseph, and Helen M. McCadden. *Félix Varela: Torch Bearer from Cuba*. 2nd edition. San Juan, Puerto Rico: Félix Varela Foundation, 1984.

Miller, Kerby A. *Emigrants and Exiles: Ireland and the Irish Exodus to North America.* New York: Oxford University Press, 1985.

Morris, Edmund. *The Rise of Theodore Roosevelt.* New York: Ballantine Books, 1980.

Sacks, Howard, and Judith Sacks. *Way Up North in Dixie.* Washington, DC: Smithsonian Institution Press, 1996.

Woodham-Smith, Cecil. *The Great Hunger.* New York: Harper & Row, 1962.

Italian

Ewen, Elizabeth. *Immigrant Women in the Land of Dollars: Life and Culture on the Lower East Side, 1890–1925.* New York: Monthly Review Press, 1985.

Gabaccia, Donna. *From Sicily to Elizabeth Street: Housing and Social Change Among Italian Immigrants, 1880–1930.* Albany: State University of New York Press, 1984.

Kessner, Thomas. *The Golden Door: Italian and Jewish Immigrant Mobility in New York City 1880–1915.* New York: Oxford University Press, 1977.

Malpezzi, Frances M., and William M. Clements. *Italian-American Folklore.* The American Folklore Series, W. K. McNeil, general editor. Little Rock, AK: August House Publishers, Inc., 1992.

Seller, Maxine. *Ethnic Theare in the United States.* Westport, Conn.: Greenwood Press, 1983.

Silone, Ignazio. *Fontamara.* London: Jonathan Cape, 1948.

Talese, Gay. "Where Are the Italian-American Novelists?" *New York Times Book Review,* March 14, 1993.

Tricarico, Donald. *The Italians of Greewich Village.* Staten Island, NY: Center for Migration Studies, 1984.

Zucchi, John E. *The Little Slaves of the Harp: Italian Child Street Musicians in Nineteenth-century Paris, London and New York.* Montreal: McGill-Queen's University Press, 1992.

Sources of Illustrations

African/Black

p. 2a The New York Public Library, Astor, Lenox, and Tilden Foundations, Phelps Stokes, Iconography of Manhattan.

p. 2b Collections of the New-York Historical Society.

p. 6 *Harper's Weekly*, August 1, 1863.

p. 9 Collections of the New-York Historical Society.

p. 11a Collections of the New-York Historical Society.

p. 11b Collection of the Lower East Side Tenement Museum.

pp. 12, 14 Photo and Print Division, Schomburg Center for Research in Black Culture, The New York Public Library, Astor, Lenox, and Tilden Foundations.

p. 15 The Billy Rose Theatre Collection, New York Public Library for the Performing Arts, Astor, Lenox, and Tilden Foundations.

p. 17 New York Times Pictures; illustration by Al Granberg.

p. 19 Collections of the New-York Historical Society.

p. 21 Photo and Print Division, Schomburg Center for Research in Black Culture, The New York Public Library, Astor, Lenox, and Tilden Foundations.

p. 22 Museum of the City of New York.

p. 23 Artist, Nicolino Calyo. Museum of the City of New York, bequest of Mrs. J. Insley Blair.

p. 25 Collections of the New-York Historical Society.

p. 27 Collections of the New-York Historical Society.

p. 29 Collections of the New-York Historical Society.

German

p. 32 *Harper's Weekly*, November 7, 1874; Collection of the Lower East Side Tenement Museum.

p. 35 Collection of the Lower East Side Tenement Museum.

p. 37 Museum of the City of New York.

p. 40 Courtesy B'nai B'rith Archives.

p. 42 Watercolor drawing by Fritz Meyer, collection of Edward W. C. Arnold, the Metropolitan Museum of Art.

p. 43 *The* [London] *Graphic*, February 10, 1877.

p. 46 Collections of the New-York Historical Society.

p. 47 UPI/Corbis Bettman.

p. 50 Lithograph by Fr. Venino, c. 1854. The J. Clarence Davies Collection, Museum of the City of New York.

p. 51 Courtesy Edmund Gillon, Jr.

p. 52 The New York Public Library, Astor, Lenox, and Tilden Foundations.

p. 53 Courtesy Edmund Gillon, Jr.

p. 54 *King's Handbook of New York City.*

p. 56 perm. Collections of the New-York Historical Society.

p. 58 perm. Collections of the New-York Historical Society.

p. 60 perm. Collections of the New-York Historical Society.

p. 61 *The* [London] *Graphic*, February 10, 1877.

Irish

p. 64 perm. Collection of the Lower East Side Tenement Museum.

p. 66 perm. *Harper's Weekly*, September 11, 1858.

p. 67 perm. New York Public Library, Astor, Lenox, and Tilden Foundations.

p. 69 perm. *Frank Leslie's Illustrated Newspaper*, April 24, 1875.

p. 71 perm. *Harper's Weekly*, September 9, 1871.

p. 73 perm. Collections of the New-York Historical Society.

p. 75 perm. Fred F. French Company Collection, the Lower East Side Tenement Museum.

p. 76 perm. *Harper's Weekly*, July 29, 1871; Grafton, *New York in the 19th Century.*

p. 78 perm. Jacob A. Riis Collection, Museum of the City of New York.

p. 97 perm. New York Public Library, Astor, Lenox, and Tilden Foundations.

p. 81 perm. Music Collection, New York Public Library for the Performing Arts, Astor, Lenox, and Tilden Foundations.

p. 82 perm. The Billy Rose Collection, New York Public Library for the Performing Arts, Astor, Lenox, and Tilden Foundations.

p. 85 perm. Collections of the New-York Historical Society.

p. 86 perm. Museum of the City of New York.

p. 88 perm. Collection of Ruth Limmer.

p. 90 perm. *Harper's Weekly*, Grafton, *New York in the 19th Century*.

p. 92 perm. *Harper's Weekly*, Grafton, *New York in the 19th Century*.

p. 94 perm. *Harper's Weekly*, November 13, 1858; Grafton, *New York in the 19th Century*.

p. 95 perm. *New York Daily News*, June 16, 1904; New York Public Library, Astor, Lenox, and Tilden Foundations.

Chinese

p. 100 perm. Courtesy of Museum of the Chinese in the Americas.

p. 106 Collection of Ruth Limmer.

p. 107 perm. Collections of the New-York Historical Society.

p. 109a, b perm. Courtesy of Museum of the Chinese in the Americas.

p. 110 perm. Brown Brothers.

p. 112 perm. Brown Brothers.

p. 114 perm. New York Public Library, Astor, Lenox, and Tilden Foundations.

p. 115 perm. Museum of the City of New York.

p. 116 perm. Courtesy of Museum of the Chinese in the Americas.

p. 117 perm. Courtesy of Museum of the Chinese in the Americas.

p. 118 perm. Museum of the City of New York.

p. 119 perm. Lower East Side Tenement Museum.

p. 121 perm. Courtesy of Museum of the Chinese in the Americas.

Jewish

p. 134 perm. The Byron Collection, Museum of the City of New York.

p. 137 perm. *Frank Leslie's Illustrated Newspaper*, September 16, 1882, the Archives of the YIVO Institute for Jewish Research.

p. 140 perm. The New York Public Library, Astor, Lenox, and Tilden Foundations.

p. 142 perm. Seward Park Branch of the New York Public Library.

p. 144 perm. From the Archives of the YIVO Institute for Jewish Research.

p. 146 perm. From the Archives of the YIVO Institute for Jewish Research.

p. 147 perm. *Harper's Weekly*, October 2, 1875; Grafton, *New York in the 19th Century*.

p. 148 perm. Seward Park Branch of the New York Public Library.

p. 150 perm. UPI/Corbis-Bettman.

p. 155 perm. J. Clarence Davies Collection, Museum of the City of New York.

p. 158 perm. Collections of the New-York Historical Society.

p. 160 perm. Winjanda Deroo, Collection of the Lower East Side Tenement Museum.

Italian

p. 164 perm. Music Collection, New York Public Library for the Performing Arts, Astor, Lenox, and Tilden Foundations.

p. 166 perm. *Harper's Weekly*, September 13, 1873.

p. 167 perm. UPI/Corbis-Bettman.

p. 170 perm. Jacob A. Riis Collection, Museum of the City of New York.

p. 172 perm. The New York Public Library, Astor, Lenox, and Tilden Foundations.

p. 174 perm. Brown Brothers.

p. 176 perm. The New York Public Library, Astor, Lenox, and Tilden Foundations.

p. 179 perm. Billy Rose Theatre Collections, the New York Public Library for the Performing Arts, Astor, Lenox, and Tilden Foundations.

p. 182 perm. UPI/Corbis-Bettman.

p. 183 perm. UPI/Corbis-Bettman.

p. 187 perm. Collections of the New-York Historical Society.

p. 189 perm. Brown Brothers.

p. 190 perm. Courtesy Cabrini Medical Center Archives.

p. 191 perm. Collection of the Lower East Side Tenement Museum.

Index

Index

Index

Index

Index

RUTH LIMMER, editor of
Tenement Times, a publication
of the Lower East Side Tenement
Museum, is the editor of *What the
Woman Lived: Selected Letters of
Louise Bogan, 1920-1970* and
Journey Around My Room, the
mosaic autobiography of Louise
Bogan. Her introduction to Bella
Spewack's *Streets* was published
in 1995.